Stealth KM

Stealth KM

Winning Knowledge Management Strategies for the Public Sector

NIALL SINCLAIR

AMSTERDAM · BOSTON · HEIDELBERG · LONDON
NEW YORK · OXFORD · PARIS · SAN DIEGO
SAN FRANCISCO · SINGAPORE · SYDNEY · TOKYO

Butterworth Heinemann is an imprint of Elsevier

ELSEVIER

Butterworth–Heinemann is an imprint of Elsevier
30 Corporate Drive, Suite 400, Burlington, MA 01803, USA
Linacre House, Jordan Hill, Oxford OX2 8DP, UK

♾ Recognizing the importance of preserving what has been written, Elsevier prints its books on
acid-free paper whenever possible.

Library of Congress Cataloging-in-Publication Data
Sinclair, Niall.
    Stealth KM : winning knowledge management strategies for the public sector / Niall Sinclair.– 1st ed.
        p. cm.
    Includes bibliographical references and index.
    ISBN 0-7506-7931-X
    1. Knowledge management. 2. Organizational learning. I. Title.
    HD30.2.S58 2006
    658.4'038–dc22

                        2005023727

British Library Cataloguing-in-Publication Data
A catalogue record for this book is available from the British Library.

ISBN 13: 978-0-7506-7931-2
ISBN 10: 0-7506-7931-X

For information on all Butterworth–Heinemann publications
visit our Web site at www.books.elsevier.com

Printed in the United States of America
06 07 08 09 10 10 9 8 7 6 5 4 3 2 1

To my inspiration and lifelong companion, Nikki, and to my wonderful children, Patrick, Keri, Holly and Calum, who have taught me more than I could ever have imagined. And to all the friends and great people I have known, particularly those whose generosity of spirit and sharing of their wisdom have made the journey a thing of fun.

Contents

Acknowledgments   viii

Preface   ix

PART I   **KM IS DEAD, LONG LIVE KM**   I

CHAPTER 1   The Problem with Governments   3

CHAPTER 2   The Problem with Knowledge Management   13

PART II   **THE PATH OF LEAST RESISTANCE**   21

CHAPTER 3   Marketing Knowledge Management Successfully   23

CHAPTER 4   Aligning Knowledge Management with the Organization   47

CHAPTER 5   Deploying Knowledge Management in the Organization   69

CHAPTER 6   Measuring Knowledge Management in the Organization   91

PART III   **MAKING THE CONNECTION: LESSONS FROM THE FRONT LINE**   III

CHAPTER 7   Lessons Learned: Some the Hard Way   113

CHAPTER 8   Successful Knowledge Management: Case Studies from the Public Sector   133

PART IV   **THE DISAPPEARING PRESENT**   **189**

CHAPTER 9   Knowledge Management: The Next
            Generation   191

            Bibliography   199

            Index   203

ACKNOWLEDGMENTS

I would like to thank the following people: Dr. Randy Frid of the Canadian Institute of Knowledge Management, whose expertise and boundless enthusiasm for knowledge management (KM) inspired me to write this book in the first place. All those colleagues who have trodden the path of KM for many years, and whose work I referenced as a foundation for this book: Professors Mike Stankosky and Frank Calabrese of the Institute for Knowledge and Innovation at the George Washington University, Professor Michael Zack of Northeastern University, Karl Erik Sveiby, Professors Jim McKeen and Heather Smith of Queen's University's Monieson Institute, Dr. Steven Newman of NASA, Ron Simmons of the FAA, Dale Chatwin of the Australian Bureau of Statistics, Tony Burgess of the U.S. Army, Chuck Seely of Intel, and Assistant Professor Dianne Ford of Nipissing University. And finally to the many friends and work colleagues who provided me encouragement and support along the way, including Margaret Logan, Dave Evraire, Don Powell, John Cousens, Gerry Monette, Steve Spence, Richard Livesley, Lisa Mibach, Wendi Cutts, John Vancea, and especially to my longtime friend Derek Rice, for the incalculable hours of fun we have shared together over the last 40 years.

PREFACE

For the last few years I have worked for the Canadian government and prior to that I worked in the private sector for more than 25 years. I started working back in the days when computing was called *data processing*, and the PC belonged to the realms of science fiction. In those days, information technology (IT) was the emerging wave of the future, and knowledge management (KM) was an unheard of subject. What mattered most to organizations in those days was how powerful their computers were, not how powerful their knowledge was, or what the value of their intellectual capital was.

During my career I have seen a number of new business trends emerge, from self-directed work teams through total quality management and on to information management (IM) and beyond. One of the hottest new business disciplines to emerge during that time has been KM. Over the last 10 to 15 years KM has held out much promise as the way forward for organizations trying to respond effectively to the emergence of the knowledge economy. The learning organization, one which holistically applies its knowledge and recognizes the value of its knowledge assets, is now the Holy Grail for many.

The government of Canada, and I would expect most governments around the world, are desperate to improve the quality of the services they deliver and their image with the citizens they serve and the media who endlessly scrutinize them. Since the new millennium, I have seen the arrival of many new Canadian government initiatives, all heralded with much fanfare and aimed at improving the way that government works. KM has not been one of those initiatives, at least not yet. So far KM has not found its appropriate level within Canadian government departments and agencies, and despite some early adopters it shows no signs of taking off any time soon. Yet, if you look at it closely, KM is probably the single best hope for successfully moving the monolith of government towards a new and improved business model, one that can better respond to the information age demands of an online and computer-savvy generation.

Governments seem to have an endless capacity for self-reflection and angst, yet are they really performing any worse than any other large and complex organization? It seems to me that throughout the years I have been a public servant, the public sector has believed that the best way for it to succeed in changing the way it operates is to try and emulate the private sector. Given that there are undoubtedly many fine examples within the private space for the public sector to emulate, there are probably an equal number of disaster stories that do not bear repeating, as the recent debacle of Enron emphasized. In fact, having been on both sides of the sector fence, I believe there are many areas where the private sector could actually learn much from the way that the public sector operates.

Over the last few years I have heard from many subject experts, read many books, and listened to many lectures on the subject of KM. It occurred to me recently that most available knowledge on the subject comes from those who are in the private sector or academia and that there is little, if anything, available from within the public sector itself, hence my decision to write this book. Others have already discussed, dissected, and defined KM from every imaginable angle. I will not retread the path they have already worn. This book will be more about winning stratagems and practical ways to embed KM into any organization, but particularly those in the public sector.

The concept of effecting real and lasting change in large, bureaucratic organizations through working *under the radar* or in *stealth mode* was the inspiration for what you will read.

For those of you of a more minimalist nature, I have included a summary section at the end of each chapter that distills the work into short and digestible sound bytes and action items to help you prioritize what needs paying attention to, and what needs to be done.

Stealth KM is as much about an attitude of mind as it is about a new way to implement KM, and I would be the first to admit that not every organization, or KM practitioner, will feel comfortable with such an approach. However, this book contains plenty of practical advice that is equally applicable whether you are adopting a stealth-type approach or are going about KM in a more traditional way. I hope you will find it useful and instructive and that the lessons learned and strategies for success it reflects may find a home in all sectors and with all KM practitioners.

PART I
KM IS DEAD, LONG LIVE KM

ONE

The Problem with Governments

GOVERNMENT, IN ITS VERY ESSENCE, IS OPPOSED TO ALL INCREASE
IN KNOWLEDGE. ITS TENDENCY IS ALWAYS TOWARD PERMANENCE AND
AGAINST CHANGE.

H. L. Mencken

I am not entirely sure that I would endorse Mencken's bleak assessment of those who run the organization known as *Government Incorporated*. However, I suspect that he speaks for the frustrated citizen in all of us, and I personally have seen my fair share of tendencies toward permanence and against change in the public sector. Without any such behavioral traits to encumber it, the business world is undergoing a profound shift in thinking and behaviour based on the fact that knowledge is now being seen as a corporate asset: an asset that needs to be managed and exploited where possible for the benefit of the organization. This changing corporate landscape is having an effect on the way that governments perceive their own need to start managing their intellectual capital. This shift has been motivated by the recognition that society is changing and that the knowledge-economy is no longer a futurist's prediction, but rather a reality that needs to be contended with, as citizens now expect their government to share and use institutional and employee knowledge to improve services and products. This means that we are also changing the very nature of our work in line with this new expectation. Accompanying this change is a new level of stress engendered by the need to reconcile our emerging understanding of how things will work in our future world with the way they currently work in a world we created from a very different set of assumptions and understanding. For example, the youngest member of a recent Team Canada mission to China was the 12-year-old chief executive officer (CEO) of an Internet design and development company. Somehow all our prejudices and presumptions kick into overdrive when we see something like that. What could a 12-year-old possibly know about the business world, running a company, or even life itself? The truth is probably more than we might imagine. He is our genetic blueprint for the 21st century, a true child of the electronic age, hot-wired, tech-savvy, and intuitively at home with cyber-, hyper-, and any other space that comes his way.

Looking at the way we all work in such an interconnected fashion, it sometimes seems that we are collectively moving toward system overload at warp speed. Change comes at us on a daily basis, instant connectivity to anywhere in the world is the norm, and we now live in a global village in the truest sense. We may be sitting in our office watching the snow pile up outside, or lying on a beach in some sunny resort, but the aspects of connectivity in a virtual world are the same. We are instantly accessible and accountable and our sense of time and space is altered accordingly. Our work changes constantly, the age of the knowledge worker has been declared as a new paradigm, and success lies in how well we can share, learn, and collaborate with others rather than in how well we keep things for our own purposes and personal advantage.

Knowledge management (KM) is the compass to help us navigate through this uncharted sea as we set sail toward the promised land of *e-everything*.

The way work is organized is also changing, and how government's organize their existing intellectual capital will help determine our future view of them as knowledge-enabled organizations. The old, bureaucratic, hierarchic, organizational stovepipes present too many barriers to effective learning environments. There are just too many constraints and controls to allow knowledge and information to move freely. The ability to capture and organize knowledge about work processes and best practices across these silos will be a key success factor for KM. E-government will reinvent the processes necessary to deliver service to citizens. As that happens, it will become apparent that the old stovepipes are no longer tenable. This sharing and interconnectivity is known as *horizontality of knowledge*. Knowledge will move within, and across, many departments as partnering becomes essential to government's ability to deliver services. However, as an old German proverb states, "To change and to change for the better are two different things." Large institutions are cumbersome in nature and slow to react to change. With the transformation from the postindustrial society to the age of cyberspace, it has become increasingly difficult for governments to adapt or respond to change at the speed that citizens are demanding. They need to find a level for change that is appropriate within the known constraints of time and resources, both human and financial. Where will they find the best returns for investing in change? What skills and abilities are required? What training, education, and recruitment programs are needed? Governments will need to be prepared for the challenges of knowledge retention and dissemination as this generation of public servants makes way for the new one.

A crucial success factor to enabling this change and delivering on new on-line services will be the government's capacity to manage its corporate knowledge. The very credibility of the public service is at stake. To achieve a level of success, public servants will need a sustainable infrastructure of standards, practices, policies, and technology enablers and the right skills to help manage the knowledge needed to support program and service delivery. Government is, and always has been, in the knowledge business, and the extent to which it manages its knowledge effectively, and holds itself accountable at the same time, will mark the extent to which it continues to be a responsive, responsible, and connected government on behalf of its citizenry. A good example of this change of emphasis is the announcement by the United Kingdom (UK) government regarding the KM National Project (see Chapter 8 on KM Case Studies) as part of its e-government agenda. They see KM as a key element of their initiative to change and modernize the way that government does business and believe that they need to provide a consistent approach to the way that KM is implemented across all local authorities.

The themes of the KM National Project are those that inform most KM projects:

- The need to leverage the role of KM in the search for better services, products, and work practices.
- The need to encourage collaboration and sharing activities.
- The need to facilitate individual and community learning and knowledge-growth.

The real wonder of this initiative is that there is one at all. Even 5 years ago, such a focus on a governmental level of KM activity was almost unheard of, and apart from one or two early adopters, most governmental KM activity was of the stated intention, rather than the actual implementation, variety. The high-profile nature of the KM National Project gives hope that the whole public sector dynamic around KM may be shifting, and that KM can find its appropriate level at last.

Despite this ray of hope, I suspect that most public sector organizations are still mired in the same old problems of lack of understanding of where KM might fit and lack of appreciation of how best to apply it. During the 2 years I worked at Public Works and Government Services Canada, we had two new deputy ministers, two complete reorganizations, four departmental reviews (two internal, two external), and endless changes in the ranks of our senior management. Not much room there to get senior managers excited about the prospect of KM. In fact, given the high turnover rate of those folks, it was painfully apparent to me that it probably was not even worth the effort of trying to get anyone at the senior level onside with the concepts of KM, and this despite the generally held belief that it is essential to have a senior champion in the organization if you want to succeed at KM. Sound familiar? The only response I can give is that it would be wise to assume that this state of affairs will always be the norm and that what is required is a new approach to embedding KM into organizations.

It is also apparent that despite all the bellyaching and wringing of hands that accompanies such upheaval, this is very much the normal state of affairs in any organization. In fact, I suspect this is a fair reflection of the state of affairs that has predominated throughout my many years in the workforce. We always believe things are worse than ever and that we are incapable of coping with the demands that work is placing on us. This leads us to the unhappy yet somehow reassuring thought that things must have been better previously. Wrong. Things have always been this way, ever since the pharaoh's chief architect started hitting the sauce as the pyramid project fell apart because of incompetence, laziness, and greed, we have struggled to maintain an even strain in the face of the demands of the work we do. The reason? Humans are obviously not hardwired to do anything without feeling a sense of resentment at the circumstances that prevail. The truth is that many would prefer to be doing anything else rather than having to work for a living. Consequently, that sense of inherent unfairness becomes a major obstacle to achieving a happy and balanced approach to the work we do. This condition will only grow as the pursuit of leisure and the ability to live new and exciting lives vicariously through the Internet becomes the norm.

What this means from a business perspective is that employers are no longer holding all the cards in the employer—employee equation. The way we perceive the rules of employment has undergone a huge shift as employees become aware that the knowledge they possess is actually the crucial factor in the employer—employee relationship. The tech boom of the 1990s brought this new relationship into sharp focus, with employers going to almost absurd lengths to attract prospective employees. Since the burst of the technology bubble things have settled down somewhat, but you can rest assured that they will never go back to the way they were. When I started work, people still thought about a job as possibly being a job for life. Today that thought seems antiquated and unrealistic. Yet, if you look at the way the public service is structured, you will probably find many public servants who have either worked in public service all their lives, or are expecting to do so. In other words, job security seems to be an expectation in the face of all reality. Because of this paradigm, governments seem to be businesses modeled after a reality that no longer exists. They are huge, stifled in layers of bureaucracy, glacial in their ability to change, and driven by policies and political correctness rather than by intuition and innovation. However, depending on where you work, and whom you work with, none of these issues is the reality of many government workers today. I have seen as much intelligence, innovation, business savvy, hard work and ownership of the issues in the public service as I ever witnessed in the private sector. So why is it seemingly so hard to make KM a success in the public sector? One of the major problems is that most managers do just not see KM as being sexy. Selling KM to management is similar to selling maintenance or energy-conservation projects. These mundane endeavors often elicit a big yawn because they are a bit indirect and intangible compared with other ways of investing the organization's money. Accordingly, KM needs to be better positioned in the organization if it is going to flourish.

The first impediment to delivering KM solutions is that many senior managers in the government would like to mold the public sector into a single organizational entity, one that follows the same rules, the same business goals, and the same business architecture. The rationale seems to be that if everyone operated in this singular and controlled fashion, there would be a big payback in terms of efficiencies and better service levels. After all, this model has worked well in large private sector organizations, such as Siemens with over 450,000 employees worldwide, so why would it not work in the Canadian public sector of only 250,000 employees? This attempt to create a Canada Inc. is well meaning, but doomed to failure. The structure of the Canadian government, or any other government for that matter, does not lend itself to this kind of a unified existence. There is no Bill Gates at the top or chairman of Canada, Inc. saying "make it so," with all employees dutifully follow the dictates laid down to them.

Governments are fragmented and disconnected entities, with many territorial, organizational, and cultural barriers in the way of such a well-ordered existence. Some governments have used this unified approach successfully, usually in response to some singular outcome such as moving government services on-line, and some have refined the approach to target some particular business objective, such as the UK government's KM National Project. However, if most governments wanted to effect such a change, they would need to completely restructure themselves on the basis of a new set of business imperatives such as single accountability for dealing with a single business issue, not the multidepartmental approach we normally see. Such a total restructuring of the way things currently work, is not something we are likely to see anytime soon. It would probably be much more effective to allow the public sector to develop along the lines of a business entity in the private sector. Give departments a mandate to deliver a service, or services, and let them determine how best to deliver on that mandate without undue interference. Then let them operate like any service provider in the private sector, with its shareholders (its citizens) judging its performance and mandating it to make any necessary changes to improve that performance. Too far-fetched to happen? Not necessarily, as the new on-line service imperative is allowing for a very similar evolution—an evolution that is beginning to allow government organizations to perceive the value proposition of KM, which is where the biggest opportunity for KM in the public sector resides.

TAKE-AWAY MENU

Here are five things (opportunities and solutions) worth remembering about governments and knowledge management:

1. Although governments at all levels throughout the world have now realized that they will need to manage their knowledge base, most still see this need purely through the demographic lens of a retiring boomer-generation workforce and the need to replace that knowledge loss.

2. Most governments seem to be making an effort to understand the need for KM from a strategic standpoint, but few if any have connected those strategic approaches

to practical outcomes such as organizational realign-
ment built around knowledge demands and flows or
reengineered and knowledge-enabled business processes
built in response to specific citizen-based knowledge
requirements.

3. E-government's requirement for the delivery of new
    on-line services requiring increasingly collaborative
    work habits and outcomes is a huge opportunity for
    making KM relevant to business owners and managers.

4. Avoid large enterprise-scale initiatives aimed at homog-
    enizing government operations, instead focus wherever
    possible on talking and working with business owners and
    middle managers who have sufficient resources to fund
    KM activity in programs and projects.

5. Keep KM activity on as small a scale as is realistic and keep
    it in alignment with business manager's goals, objectives,
    and measures of success.

TWO

The Problem with Knowledge Management

SPECIES OF KNOWLEDGE ARE SCATTERED THROUGH A VAST EMPTINESS
OF IGNORANCE, AND EVERYTHING DEPENDS UPON HOW SOLID THE
INDIVIDUAL SPECIES OF KNOWLEDGE ARE, AND ON HOW POWERFULLY
LINKED AND COORDINATED THEY ARE WITH ONE ANOTHER.

Thomas Sowell

I suspect if you asked the question, "Does knowledge matter?" of most people in organizations today the answer would be a resounding yes. However, the real question we should be asking ourselves is, "Does knowledge matter to our business?" and if we did ask it, I think we would find a very different response. I believe it is because we have not yet made the connection between what people intuitively know and what organizations intuitively do. Knowledge management (KM) is not well understood or properly valued by the leaders of most organizations. We need to do a much better job of demystifying it as a business discipline and find a way to show that it is neither elitist nor impractical. In fact, KM is anything but a new concept: It has been practiced since mankind first formed into communities. We learn from our parents about the world. We learn from our communities at school, work, or home, on a continual basis. And most of all, we learn from our own experiences about what works and what mistakes we need to avoid in the future. We are all in the knowledge-exchange business and spend much of our lives learning from others and sharing our experiences and lessons learned with them in exchange. Without sound KM, humans would not be able to function as they do, and we would not have achieved all the amazing and wonderful things we have done. Thus, it was only going to be a matter of time before someone stuck a label on what we have been doing intuitively forever, declared it to be new and innovative, and figured out how to make a living from telling others about it. The problem with that is that it lends KM an aura of being new and different, and consequently difficult, instead of being intuitive and easy to understand. Because of this perception, KM has struggled to find its corporate comfort zone.

Despite this obstacle, what has begun to take place over the last 10 to 15 years is a new emphasis on KM as a business concept, one that holds the promise of a better way of doing business. For this reason, governments around the world are looking at KM as a potential means of managing their human capital. The focus on KM is because governments are going to be especially impacted by the problem of changing demographics due to the impending retirement from the workforce of the baby-boomer generation. However KM is counterintuitive in relation to how government organizations have traditionally functioned. The average government office functions through a strict adherence to policies, rules, and hierarchy—not at all how KM tends to work best. KM flourishes when practitioners find a strong ratio-nale for it, usually through the identification and formation of communities of interest or practice, and then allow knowledge to be exchanged and used without much regard to formal processes. Therein lies the crux of the problem for the average public sector organization: KM holds out much promise as a means to work more effectively, but it seems that there is a significant pain barrier to face up to if it is to be successfully implemented. In fact, it needs to be understood that many people in an organization will not benefit from KM in their daily work, and will not ever have a need to implement KM in their work processes. It definitely is not a cure-all to all known organizational problems and that is one of the issues that KM practitioners need to consider in their endeavors. KM is more about how much an individual or community trades in knowledge and how much their job function is dependent on the need to share knowledge and collaborate with others.

As Price Pritchett (1994) points out in his excellent book, *New Work Habits for a Radically Changing World,* embracing change and developing the work habits needed for success in the information age has become the success mantra for many organizations in both private and public sectors. This requires them to change their operational models of business if they want to be successful and that means change management is an essential component of any knowledge-based initiative. A culture of learning and knowledge sharing does not happen by accident. Old ways of hoarding knowledge as a means of exercising power and control need to be exposed as inappropriate, grounded in outdated management practices, and having no place in the public service of the 21st century. If that goal cannot be achieved, governments will face major problems in streamlining their processes and ensuring better services to their citizens. To effect change, you must invest time in learning with, and from, others; building a value system of trust and openness with them; and, above all, learning to work horizontally not vertically, whether with co-workers or virtual team members. For knowledge sharing to become a reality, you must create a climate of trust. You cannot empower someone that you do not trust and who does not trust you. For government, the rationale for doing this is to deploy better knowledge at the point of service for the benefit of their client, the citizen.

If someone asked you to identify the average government's most valuable asset, what would your answer be? Their funds, buildings, fixtures and fittings, or computer hardware? All have their own value, yet strategically the most valuable assets are those of knowledge, the intellectual capital of the people in the public service. Thomas Stewart (2001) in his book, *Intellectual Capital*, says, "The primary purpose of human capital is innovation, whether of new products and services, or of improvement in business processes." So one of the problems for those interested in advancing KM in the public sector is how to sell it on the basis of its organizational value and how to achieve sufficient attention and resources to give it a realistic chance of being a success.

There are enough experts and vendors in the field of KM to populate a small country, and yet no one has figured *it* out successfully or managed to come up with the winning formula to be applied in governments across the world. I find this greatly reassuring as it tells me that no one knows the answer to the question, "what is KM?" I believe this is because we are all experts in KM, and every time someone practices KM, they do so from a different perspective, for different personal or business reasons, and to satisfy a myriad of different requirements. Accordingly, I will spend no time in attempting a definition for KM, and I believe that any definition that works for any organization is the right one. In fact, the only sure recipe for success in attempting to sell the concept of KM in organizations is to find out what the business requirement for doing KM is and define it in those terms. For example, here is how we described KM in Public Works and Government Services Canada (PWGSC),

A discipline and organizational strategy for ensuring that corporate knowledge is identified, captured, created, shared and used to improve and maintain the services that PWGSC delivers to its clients.

This definition, based on departmental strategic goals and objectives, covered all the necessary bases and PWGSC's commitment to improve its delivery of our services to their clients. A rule of thumb you can apply to definitions is the following: If you can choose anyone in the organization, even someone who has never heard of KM, and they understand what the definition is, and how it applies to their business issues, it is probably the right one.

So what is needed to address this issue of organizational indifference toward implementing KM tools and techniques? First, do not panic, things are not as bad as they may sometimes seem. What KM has got going for it is that people intuitively *get it*, if it is positioned as just another part of good business management practices, one that does not demand a lot of additional workload, and one that is already being practiced by many in the organization, even if they do not attach a KM label to it. If business managers and employees can see KM in that light, you do not really need to *sell* it to the senior strata of managers, as the bottom-up approach is always going to go the distance. The concept of the Trojan Horse is one that is embraced by those who want to change things by stealth, and KM is an excellent prospect for just such an approach in most organizations.

Many KM practitioners and managers seem to believe that it is their mission to be the evangelists for this new business discipline of KM in their organizations. The truth is, they would be much better served in finding how KM can fit into a supporting role for something that is already an established and well-regarded business discipline in the organization, project management for instance. Most new projects will have all the right ingredients in place for providing KM with a platform on which to shine, or at least on which to play a strong supporting role. This theme of the *path of least resistance* is one that I will elaborate on later in the book. In summary, it involves finding a home for KM activity in your organization, the level or degree of engagement is irrelevant. This is all about finding KM's fit and relevance to the business, and if it means that KM is subsumed to some degree by another discipline, then so be it. I personally have no time for those who think in an all-or-nothing kind of mentality and who see anything except total acceptance of KM as some sort of failure. It has taken IM many years to become part of the conversation at the senior managers table—do they really expect the business world to wholeheartedly accept and endorse KM overnight? If so, they are in for a long wait. I would much rather have KM activities occurring all over the place, playing a supportive role, and being valued by those involved, than hoping it will sweep all before it in a moment of organizational epiphany.

The real secret to making KM successful in any organization is to understand its irrelevance to most business employees. This does not mean that KM is irrelevant, far from it. In fact, it may lead to some of the most significant advances in effectiveness and efficiency that any business unit will ever see. However, too often, KM initiatives have founded on the rock of intransigence, because the KM community believes they understand the discipline and know how it should be implemented, rather than being prepared to relinquish, or at least diminish, their role of subject—expert. The message is clear: Help the business find KM's relevance and let them own it and customize it any way they want. Let them bend and change KM into a shape that fits their view of the way it should work. If they are smart, they will know the limits of their capabilities around KM and look to partner with those that are in the know. In other words, start with the view that there are no rights and wrongs involved in doing KM work: Any approach is acceptable if it helps KM find a place at the corporate table.

This cavalier approach to implementing KM may seem like a slap in the face to those who have devoted their careers to learning about KM and promoting its virtues to all and sundry and to those who believe there is a proper way to implement it. It should not be. After all, without those evangelists no one would really be talking about KM as a business discipline at all. And, their skills and expertise will be more in demand than ever once business units start the KM voyage themselves. But the truth is, KM is still mainly seen as being somehow academic and ivory tower in its thinking, somewhat arcane in its competency, and above all somewhat removed from the day-to-day realities of the business world. If we ever want to change those perceptions, we have to find a winning formula for selling and delivering KM to the business and then allow them to implement it in a way that is meaningful and relevant to them.

TAKE-AWAY MENU

Here are five things worth remembering about KM in any organization:

1. Keep things in proportion and remember that the term *KM* is probably meaningless to most of the people you are likely to deal with in any organization.

2. Focus on demystifying KM at every opportunity and show in as many ways as is possible how practical and relevant KM can be in helping to achieve business goals and objectives.

3. To begin with, find where the organization's subject—experts and communities of practice exist and start explaining KM's value proposition to that audience in

terms they can understand and be able to communicate onward.

4. Whenever you talk to any audience about KM, emphasize the creation of a value system of openness and trust as an important component of KM outcomes.

5. Remember that no one knows all the answers about what KM looks like, so do not be afraid to go in different directions depending on the way that business owners perceive its value to their business.

PART II

THE PATH OF LEAST RESISTANCE

THREE

Marketing Knowledge Management Successfully

A SINGLE CONVERSATION ACROSS THE TABLE WITH A WISE MAN IS
WORTH A MONTH'S STUDY OF BOOKS.

Chinese Proverb

If we have always managed knowledge, why do we think that knowledge management (KM) is something new? That question is one that continues to baffle me, and what it tells me is that KM is still searching for a happy place where it can stop being the new kid on the block and just get on with what it has always been doing, without the spotlight of organizational attention blinding it. As any good salesperson can tell you: It is not about the product; it is about how you sell it. In this case, you are looking to sell the organization on the need to value and manage its knowledge with the same diligence it manages its other organizational assets.

Therefore one of the most fundamental steps for anyone tasked with implementing KM is that of setting a realistic expectation level within their organization. It is vital that everyone understands that KM is not a silver bullet and that it is just another business management discipline that succeeds or fails dependent on how much attention is given it. The message is simple: KM is about making better decisions together, nothing more.

There are many individuals involved with knowledge-based processes and activities in government apart from those we would view as having a traditional interest or responsibility for KM activity, such as communities of practice members or managers accountable for delivering KM to the organization. Examples of the new breed of public servant working from a KM perspective would be front-line officers, subject experts, program officers, cluster managers, information synthesists, consultation staff, communications officials, policy officials, common services integrators, and middle managers (from *Archetypes of the Network Age: Articulating the New Public Service Reality*, a report by Public Works and Government Services, Canada). Those engaged in attempting to embed KM activity into the public service will need to first become entrepreneurs and learn how to sell the concept of KM. Selling KM presents some interesting challenges, and your chances of success are very much tied to how well you understand your market and its needs. For example, try to sell the basic concept of KM to senior managers and they'll invariably tune-out. They see KM as too indirect and intangible, and aren't comfortable with its apparent lack of structure and visible return on investment (ROI) indicators. However, if you tell senior managers that the maturity of their organization from the perspective of exploiting the value of their organizational knowledge rates a one on a scale of one to five, they will invariably show more interest. This is because you have just described KM to them in terms of organizational performance measurements that they understand. However, much of the understanding of what KM can actually do for organizations is still at a fairly low level, often only seen through the eyes of practitioner, academic research, and white papers or from the perspective of small initiatives scattered throughout the business. At the same time, KM has to compete for corporate resources with other business areas such as information technology (IT), and to a lesser degree, information management (IM). However, one of the things that the IT community has learned to do over the last 20 years is how to properly market itself. If KM wants to raise its profile, or at least the level of understanding around the discipline, it needs to find ways to better market itself to the organization.

Why Market Knowledge Management?

Knowledge managers understand the benefits that KM can bring to any organization, but until they have some backing from that organization, they are mainly going to be crying in the wilderness. To achieve this backing there needs to be a mechanism for communicating KM's potential to employees and for building a supportive and collaborative environment for disseminating information and opportunities for improvement around it. A KM marketing campaign accomplishes this goal. As Karl-Erik Sveiby (1997) states in *The New Organizational Wealth*, knowledge organization managers need a strategy for personnel markets just as much as they need a strategy for customer markets.

Marketing is seen by many as being no more than a necessary evil, or even an unnecessary one in many cases. However, if you think of it in the context of your communications needs, it can be seen as an essential and positive component of your KM game plan. And while the competitive context is absent from the public sector model, it is still apparent that marketing skills are needed to achieve the following:

- Better position KM as a product.
- Understand business client needs.
- Build partnerships and business relationships.

- Improve customer awareness.
- Provide customer satisfaction.

The goal of any marketing campaign is to ensure that the thing you are marketing (the product or service) meets the needs of its audience in terms of such things as functionality, quality, and cost. Successful marketing requires that you properly identify the needs of your target audience and look to increase audience satisfaction by delivering against those needs. *Needs* is the operative word here, as meeting the needs of the customer should be the only rationale for any KM marketing that you undertake.

Many marketing specialists have adapted Maslow's Hierarchy of Needs as a baseline to assess organizational needs levels, particularly the concept of lower-order needs needing to be continually addressed to successfully progress to meeting higher-level needs. Therefore, before proceeding with your marketing strategy you will need to identify, understand, and classify the different needs of your prospective audience. In the marketing world, needs are often defined as one of the following types: already present; latent; and absent or weak. If the need is already present, the target audience already believes that it needs a product or a service to help it move from its current state to a different or desired state. If the need is latent then the target audience needs to be reminded of a previously established, or identified, need. If the need is absent or weak, the need for your product or service will first have to be established, and the target audience will then need to be sold on the efficacy of any proposed product or service.

Once the type of need has been identified, the marketing's job is to ensure that the product or service you are offering is the one selected to meet that need. To ensure this outcome, the target audience will need to be made aware of the features of the product or service, for example, what it involves, where and how it would be used, and/or what are the expected outcomes of its use. This raising of awareness in your audience is known as *brand awareness*.

Finally, it is necessary to create what is known as brand attitude. Brand attitude refers to the way that an audience reacts to a brand and its ability to meet their business requirements. Your audience's attitude may be either favorable or unfavorable, but that the attitude has to be favorable before that audience is likely to be willing to purchase your product or service. In fact, marketing gurus will tell you that brand attitudes must be specific to a current need to be worth acting upon.

Typically, the last steps in the marketing process are aimed at assisting the audience to take action on the purchase and use of a product or service, usually known as *brand purchase intention*. This stage may not be necessary, as would be the case in a normal market campaign, because most business units will be quite capable of making a go/no-go decision concerning possible KM deployment. However, it is always a good idea to be ready and available to help with any business unit's planning and decision-making processes regarding the potential use of KM. In fact, given the lack of qualified KM specialist knowledge in most organizations, this is quite likely to be the norm.

Challenges to Successful Marketing

One of the major challenges for any marketing activity is to clearly identify the target audience or audiences. Each organization will have a unique KM demographic, and your KM marketing plan will vary depending on where you decide to focus. It may make most sense to focus on each business unit as a unique environment, one that requires a unique set of KM activities. Or, perhaps you decide to focus on the wider organization and design your KM activities with that in mind. Whether you go with the micro or macro view, there are likely to be a number of similar audiences represented in either view (e.g., senior managers, business managers, communities of practice, client service teams, project managers, etc.). Also, remember that whatever you eventually identify as your audience, both individual and group needs are always in a state of flux, and you will need to constantly check whether audience KM needs are being met by you, and if not, you will need to fine-tune your marketing strategy accordingly. This may sound onerous, but it is all about ensuring KM activity is seen as being relevant and in touch with the business. If you do not demonstrate KM's relevance to the organization up front, then the longer-term prognosis for KM activity will not be good.

Once you have identified your audience, you can begin the task of identifying KM needs. The biggest challenges you face here are that the benefits of deploying KM tools and techniques are likely to be weak or unidentified in most business units. In fact it is highly likely that few, if any, employees will be aware of what kind of activities KM provides and what kind of business needs could be addressed through using KM techniques and practices. However you wish to describe KM to your audience—whether as a service, a competency, a process, a culture, or whatever—a major part of the process of the identification of needs will be the promotion of KM activities and outcomes and the linking of those outcomes to the needs of the business community. You must make KM seem relevant and practical to your audience, and convince them of its potential value, or else they will never express a need for it. You will need to think from the perspective of the business units and senior mangers to define success in terms of business outcomes. This is really retro-engineering, looking at the desired end state and then trying to identify critical content and knowledge-sharing processes that would help achieve it. Remember to keep an open mind about this identification: What you think of as classic KM activity may not be what your business managers are thinking of as their KM needs. However, KM is broad and deep enough to fit into many different business domain requirements, regardless of whether they are based on content, data, or information.

Without creating a value proposition for KM, and allowing business units to find a fit for it in their business goals and objectives, it will be almost impossible to create any brand awareness and attitude. In fact, one of the issues that you are likely to face in seeking a positive brand attitude for KM is setting a realistic level of expectation around KM activity in the organization. This is a delicate balancing act you are attempting—while you are trying to create enthusiasm for KM in create a level of need, and thereby create awareness, you do not want to overpromise on what KM will do for the organization. The corporate landscape is littered with graveyards full of dead KM initiatives, many of which died as a result of unrealistic expectations.

There are a number of areas of possible focus when developing brand awareness, and when trying to achieve a positive brand attitude:

- Seeing if there is an executive spokesperson willing to promote KM as a desired business activity, and willing to be seen as the corporate KM lead;
- Outreach and awareness sessions with individuals, project teams, management teams, and communities of practice or at organizational forum and other corporate-wide meetings;
- Promotional activities such as KM days, knowledge fairs, knowledge contests, library days, and rewards and recognition ceremonies for KM practitioners;
- Communications around successful KM, from internal and external perspectives. The identification of internal projects and successes will go a long way to demystifying KM and in making it become real for employees. At the

same time, the communication of external success stories
and best practices can provide insight and stimulation to
employees looking for ways to work more effectively;
- Creating satisfied customers through KM work. This is
  the single greatest positive impact you can make for KM in
  your organization. Having a business partner become an
  evangelist for KM is what you should target above anything
  else.

HOW TO MARKET KNOWLEDGE MANAGEMENT EFFECTIVELY

Research shows that to be successful, entrepreneurs who face
the reality of a dormant or nonexistent market tend to focus on
the building of a new market and on the shaping of its needs. To
some extent, this is creating the market and its need, through
declaring it to be so, and through a degree of self-promotion
achieved by raising awareness and shaping perceptions around
the virtues of what you are doing. To succeed with this approach,
it is necessary to have a well-refined sense of what a winning
outcome for your strategy will look like. In other words, what is
the end game you are after? This is where an understanding of
the organization's knowledge needs is crucial to your success.
Planning for the required responses to the various levels of
corporate knowledge needs is what the strategy will be all about.

One of the first issues to be resolved is what to call KM in
your organization. This may sound like an esoteric argument,
but the name you choose can have a profound impact on how
you position KM work in the organization and on its subsequent
chances of being a success. For whatever reason, the term *KM*
is not being embraced wholeheartedly by senior mangers and
organizational planners. In fact, I have been amazed over the
last few years to find the lengths to which some practitioners have
gone to disguise the fact that they are doing KM at all. If actual

KM practitioners are being forced to adopt this approach, it tells you that they do not have any faith in the marketability of the term *KM* and that they are seeing it as a potential liability as they try to embed the organizational changes necessary to move management of knowledge forward.

Much as the initial reaction might be to think, "What's in a name?" It appears that the answer is, quite a lot. If you want to have any chance of a successful outcome for a KM initiative, it is vital to conduct some sort of a marketing campaign around it. What you actually call it is, to some extent, irrelevant. The best approach is to latch onto a strategic organizational objective and use a label for KM in the context of that objective. When I worked at Public Works and Government Services Canada (PWGSC), we ended up using the term *knowledge mobilization*. This worked on several levels: It was aligned in terms of the most senior managers' accountability accords; it was a very proactive and descriptive label, one that seemed to imply something dynamic and worthwhile; it was easily understood by everyone in the organization at expert and novice levels of KM understanding and everywhere in between; it sounded "new" yet expressed an age-old business activity; and last, it kept the initials of KM intact and thus was somehow seen as being more acceptable to the true die-hard practitioners in the organization.

The Marketing Plan

Whatever label you decide upon for your KM initiative, it is equally important to have a compelling storyline in terms of a marketing plan. The plan needs to be smart enough to address business-level concerns about activities, possible resource implications and other organizational impacts, and still be flexible enough to allow for some wiggle room as things unfold.

First, you will need to understand the varying degrees of knowledge needs that you will encounter within the organization. To manage these needs and plan a strategy around them, it would be useful to divide them along some arbitrary, yet fairly broad, lines. Practitioners seem to agree that there are probably three main categories of knowledge needs in most organizations: basic, enabling, and strategic.

Basic Needs

The organization has a number of knowledge needs relating to its ability to operate successfully. These operationally based knowledge requirements might include the following: knowledge for solving day-to-day business problems; knowledge to prevent business problems from occurring; knowledge around how business processes work; and knowledge of client's needs and how to address them. Underpinning these operational requirements are a number of knowledge-based business activities: good information management practices and techniques; data creation, storage, and extraction capacity (e.g., database administration and data marts); expertise identification activity such as knowledge mapping or knowledge directories; customer relationship management (CRM) through client service teams or CRM managers; and internal knowledge navigation aids such as knowledge portals and web sites.

Enabling Needs

The organization has a number of knowledge needs relating to its ability to achieve its tactical goals and objectives. These tactically based knowledge requirements might include the following: data mined and knowledge accumulated through the use of business intelligence tools; knowledge responsibilities embedded in business processes; knowledge dependencies identified in business processes; knowledge assets better exploited through proper sharing and reuse mechanisms; knowledge domains integrated through overarching metadata and taxonomy frameworks; desktop navigation to subject expertise through the use of knowledge directories, maps and portals; a support infrastructure that business units can use to help identify knowledge-based problems, needs, and enabling tools and techniques.

Strategic Needs

The organization has a number of knowledge needs relating to its ability to achieve its strategic goals and objectives, and to promote creativity and innovation in its workforce. These strategically based knowledge requirements might include the following: knowledge dissemination is promoted through the creation and support of teams, networks and communities; evolution toward becoming a learning organization is planned; knowledge-based activities such as sharing and re-use become part of the corporate culture.

In order to create an effective KM strategy, you should try to assess the level of success that KM is currently achieving in response to the audience's needs. This will aid in determining the initial focus for the central KM function (maybe a KM office, or Center of Competence). One way of doing this is to use an assessment tool, and there are plenty of those for you to choose from. Many of the leading consulting firms have developed tools for KM assessment. For example, Arthur Anderson, along with the APQC (American Productivity and Quality

Center), created an evaluation tool called KMAT (Knowledge Management Assessment Tool), which looks at organizational KM maturity regarding processes, leadership, culture, technology, and measurement. Microsoft on the other hand, uses a KM Value Assessment (KVA) framework based on balanced scorecard, activity-based accounting, and information economics. It measures knowledge assets, quality, and maturity in the context of performance goals (e.g., growth in patents), activity measures (e.g., white papers produced by a researcher), and behaviour measures from KM system usage records and personnel records (e.g., attending seminars, searching archives). At PWGSC we developed a KM maturity survey with the Canadian Institute of Knowledge Management (CIKM) that contained questions in the following areas: knowledge planning; knowledge retention; knowledge sharing and re-use; knowledge processes; knowledge tools; and, knowledge culture (see Chapter 6 for more details).

Whatever you decide to use, you are looking to not only guide the direction of the central KM group, but also to help business managers, and knowledge workers generally, identify areas of knowledge needs on which they should be focusing. The results of any assessment will also be helpful in deciding where to focus initial KM efforts and longer-term plans for individual business units and the organization as a whole. Although the results of any such assessment are not an exact science, they will prove useful in getting things in perspective.

So, here are some basic questions you could use for making such an initial assessment. The intention is to use the score to help guide initial KM focus and develop some longer-term KM goals. Although such an activity is an imperfect science at best, it can help you put some structure around the business environment and at the very least enable you to take the pulse of the organization (or business unit) from a KM perspective. Score two points if the answer to a question is yes, one point if

TABLE 3.1   *Assessing KM Issues and Opportunities*

	Yes	Sometimes	No
When someone requires basic information about products, customers, or other employees, can they easily get it?			
KM services are regarded highly by the business?			
The senior manager in the organization is knowledgeable about KM?			
The organization's critical information is well-organized and easy to access?			
Employees can describe KM's role in the organization?			
The central KM office is consulted about business decisions?			
The work of the central KM office is well regarded by business managers?			
The corporate Intranet/portal is considered useful by employees?			
The organization's middle management is supportive of KM?			
The CEO/Business unit leader considers KM as integral to their business strategy?			

CEO, chief executive officer; KM, knowledge management.

Adapted from *Marketing KM to the Organization* a Queens University KM Forum report (vol. 5, no. 2) by Jim McKeen and Heather Smith, 2003.

the answer is sometimes, and zero points if the answer is no (see Table 3.1). The scoring is as follows:

0–8 Points: The KM office should focus on meeting the organization's basic knowledge needs.

9–14 Points: The KM office is a competent knowledge supplier and should focus on providing knowledge services to the organization.

15—20 Points: Knowledge supply mechanisms and knowledge services are well developed, the KM office should focus on becoming a knowledge partner with the business.

Based on the three levels of corporate knowledge needs and the degree of KM maturity you see in the organization, you are ready to proceed with the marketing plan. Depending on your resource base and on the buy-in of the organization, you may choose to address all three needs levels at the same time or perhaps begin with a focus on just the tier 1 basic needs.

To help you formulate a successful approach to marketing KM, Figure 3.1 shows an overview of what the various KM objectives, strategies, and outcomes in the organization might look like. Due to the high degree of interdependency and commonality of activities and deliverables, any strategy can easily accommodate either a single- or multiple-needs—level approach. Each of the plans for the three levels will have accompanying tasks and measures that address the objectives, audience, strategies, competencies, issues and critical success factors, and, most important, the role of KM in facilitating each outcome. I will describe these in greater detail as we review the approach to each needs level.

MARKETING KNOWLEDGE MANAGEMENT FOR BASIC KNOWLEDGE NEEDS

Most organizations are at the basic knowledge level and you will likely find most of the following issues to deal with:

- Information processes are disjointed, and maybe even disconnected.
- Data are widely disseminated in multiple formats and with little or no common classification schema.

	Tier 1. Basic Knowledge Needs	Tier 2. Enabling Knowledge Needs	Tier 3. Strategic Knowledge Needs
Objectives	Establish KM Competence	Establish knowledge as a service enabler	Establish knowledge as a business imperative
Audience	Knowledge workers	Business and process managers	Senior managers
Marketing Spin	KM manages what we know	KM grows what we know	KM helps build new capabilities
Strategies	• Deliver existing information better • Partner with existing projects • Promote improved IM practices	• Establish better content integration e.g., data, records, web, corporate knowledge, etc. • Embed KM into business processes	• Help solve strategic problems • Help improve decision-making capacity • Build business capability
KM Competencies	• Analysis and packaging of information • Effective IM practices	• Knowledge analysis • Knowledge enabled business processes • E-content management	• Culture evolution • Community evolution • Service evolution
Obstacles	KM is seen as being too fuzzy to manage	KM is seen as being too broad to manage	KM is seen as being a technology issue only
Success Criteria	KM is included in any projects	KM is included from a process improvement perspective	KM strategy aligns and is integrated with business strategy
KM's Role	Knowledge supplier	Knowledge service provider	Knowledge business partner

FIGURE 3.1   *Marketing activity matrix. Adapted from McKeen and Smith, Queens University, 2003.*

- Transactional processes are silo'd and not analyzed and consolidated.
- Subject expertise is not identified or made available to all.
- Identifiable knowledge processes and practices are few and far between.

In other words, business as usual! This is a fact worth remembering, as I believe a lot of nonsense is talked about operational maturity levels in organizations and how every organization should be considering ways to move along the magic continuum that takes them to the highest level of maturity and corporate excellence. This may hold true for some, but I think the vast majority of businesses operate quite successfully at level 2 or 3 of the maturity scale. Do not get "suckered" into believing that only businesses that are performing optimally can be successful, the most businesses will never get anywhere near the rarefied air of a level 5, or even a level 4 organization. Do not despair, this is really an endless vista of opportunity for KM stretching out in front of you. The secret to success at this basic level of needs is to look for ways to ensure that existing knowledge sources are accurate and above all accessible to employees.

The following section is an overview of the main components of your marketing activity for the three need levels. This framework of knowledge needs, and their appropriate responses, will provide a solid platform for any marketing activity you undertake. The whole premise of this KM marketing strategy is to win the hearts and minds of the organization's business managers. Without that group on board, you are going to find it difficult to gain any traction for your KM strategy. As knowledge-based activity grows in your organization, along with its accompanying growth in skills and competencies, you are laying the foundations to build on for the next level. This methodical approach to marketing KM will allow it to find its proper level in the organization, and to help build the confidence and trust from the business community that you will need to achieve your agenda for transforming business processes.

Basic Needs Level

Objectives

The main objective here is to establish a basic level of organizational competence where KM is concerned. The work of KM at this level is to start building good knowledge-based practices and a consistent approach to managing knowledge assets that improves business processes and establishes KM as a valuable and trustworthy tool in the minds of business managers. This means that employees should have at least some understanding of the principles and desired outcomes of the activity of KM, and those tasked with knowledge-based accountabilities should be equipped with the basic skills necessary to address KM responsibilities in their daily work activities.

Audience

The main audience will be knowledge workers, although the wider objective of establishing a basic competence level may include many, if not all, additional employees. The first activity here will be to identify the stakeholder community, either through self-identification or through identification by managers or business owners. This may prove to be more of an obstacle than you might initially think, as many knowledge workers do not see themselves as such, or at best see knowledge as only a small component of the work they do. You will need to provide some initial guidance to help the community understand what the designation *knowledge worker* might equate to in terms of the organization. Any business unit that is process-rich, or has well-established business rules, would be a good place to focus. Support personnel, client service teams, project teams, or indeed any subject—expert community, would be good examples to highlight. However, try not to be too narrow with the focus here, as the whole point is for the organization's personnel to see themselves as being reliant on, and a provider of, knowledge.

Market Spin

This is where you will need to make the connection between what people intuitively do and what the organization needs to intuitively think about KM. The value proposition, and hence your marketing edge, is that KM is the activity that connects what the organization knows to those employees that need to know what the organization knows—building bridges between islands of knowledge, as Randy Frid of the CIKM describes it.

Engagement Strategies

Engagement here is about finding ways to help business units to exploit their information, data, and knowledge assets more effectively. Remember that at the same time you are also trying to win some hearts and minds. You will need to work with business owners to identify processes where service levels and customer expectations could be compromised by a breakdown in the flow of knowledge. Given the limited resource base of most business units, it will probably be easiest to focus on an existing project (IT probably) where you can demonstrate how KM can add value (e.g., knowledge of client's information needs and how to promote better information management practices to address those needs). Do not forget the bottom line here: You want to reinforce the brand message that KM helps the organization manage what it knows better, so keep KM's role simple and effective.

Knowledge Management Skills Needed

Really this stage is all about better IM in the organization, so the necessary KM skills are focused there. The promotion of good IM practices with a special focus on the analysis, packaging and presentation of information is what's needed.

Obstacles to Progress

There is no comfort zone established around KM yet, so promotion or marketing to the senior managers is a stretch at this point. KM is still seen as being too "soft and fuzzy," and is not yet well-enough grounded in the business to allow for any engagement at an enterprise level (e.g., major or long-term projects, culture refinement, or alignment behind corporate-wide knowledge-based infrastructure components such as metadata standards and taxonomies).

What Will Success Look Like?

Determine what success will look like when business managers look to KM to help provide the skills necessary to improve corporate information management practices.

Enabling Needs Level

Objectives

The main objective here is to establish KM as a value-added activity for business managers, one that provides knowledge services that improve business process effectiveness. As knowledge-based activities find their way into day-to-day business processes, they will promote new behaviour patterns that will begin to influence the organization's culture and start to embed knowledge capture, sharing, and reuse activity into the fabric of the organization. The outcome of this should be that KM has established itself as the provider of knowledge services to the organization.

Audience

The main audience will be anyone who is involved with the management or maintenance of business processes for the organization.

Market Spin

This is where you will need to make the connection between what the organization needs to become more effective and the capacity KM has to address those needs. The value proposition, and hence your marketing edge, is that KM adds value to the organization's business processes. In fact, part of the marketing message you are trying to impart is that KM is the only business discipline that can knowledge-enable the organization.

Engagement Strategies

Engagement here is about finding ways to help business units improve their business processes. The focus is primarily on improvement through the better management of existing knowledge and the inclusion of new knowledge. You are looking for ways to combine existing and new knowledge in ways that improve decisions and outcomes and that are shareable and reusable by all employees. Focus on more comprehensive approaches to managing information and content through formalizing workflow processes, implementing information standards and guidelines, and categorizing content through the use of metadata and classification schema.

Knowledge Management Skills Needed

Business analysis expertise will be necessary to help identify information and/or content silos. Content management skills across multiple business domains (e.g., records, documents, e-mail, Intranet, Internet, databases, etc.) will also be required. Most important of all will be business process/workflow analysis skills, as this is where you will focus for areas that could be improved through the better application of corporate knowledge. The emphasis from the corporate KM team will be on their role as the organization's knowledge broker, bringing the aforementioned skills to those business units requiring help with their processes. Remember that a collaborative and partnering mindset is an absolute must.

Obstacles to Progress

There are not many major obstacles in the way at this stage, beyond those of scope and scale. The focus is very much at the business unit level and the business process level within those units. So while the work itself is not at an enterprise level as such, what you are doing here is really laying the foundations for the longer-term strategic KM changes you are planning for the organization.

What Will Success Look Like?

Determine what success will look like when KM is seen as a crucial component of business process management and the KM group's role as corporate knowledge brokers is seen as a high-value activity by the business managers in the organization.

Strategic Needs Level

Objectives

The main objective here is to marry the business and knowledge strategies for the organization and demonstrate how KM facilitates corporate decision making and provides support to management. The intention at this level is to lever the knowledge infrastructure that has been put in place through the responses to the previous two levels of need. KM practices and techniques can be targeted at producing a creative and innovative work environment.

Audience

The main audience will be the senior managers and business leaders of the organization.

Market Spin

This is where you will need to make the connection between KM activities and the development of new organizational competencies. The value proposition, and hence your marketing edge, is that KM helps people make better decisions and therefore helps them to work more effectively.

Engagement Strategies

Engagement here is about finding ways to embed knowledge into the strategic evolution of the organization (e.g., executive education about KM's capacity to improve management decision-making capability). The focus is very much on integrating knowledge components into the organization's products, services, and customer-based interactions.

Knowledge Management Skills Needed

This stage is all about promoting collaborative approaches and solutions to enterprise-wide strategic objectives (e.g., facilitating communities, helping business units embed knowledge into products and services, and promoting innovative and creative problem solving approaches across the enterprise).

Obstacles to Progress

The main thing to avoid at this level is being too mired in the present rather than focusing on what the future state of affairs needs to be. This level is where long-term planning and vision are actually necessary and where you get the chance to push the envelope for once.

What Will Success Look Like?

Determine what success will look like when KM finds its place at the corporate planning table and is seen to be fully integrated into business strategy and decision-making by the senior managers of the organization.

TAKE-AWAY MENU

Here are five things worth remembering about marketing KM:

1. Good marketing is predicated on setting the right expectation level in the organization, so keep the message simple (e.g., *KM is about making better decisions together, nothing more*).

2. Do not position KM in a competitive organizational market space such as IT, but rather align it as a subset

activity of something already funded and under way (e.g., business process re-engineering, or program or project development).

3. Market against known customer needs and nothing else.

4. Wherever possible, market to already formed organizational entities such as business management teams, communities of practice or interest, client service teams, project managers, etc.

5. Always think from a business unit perspective, not a KM perspective, before beginning any marketing activity.

FOUR

Aligning Knowledge Management with the Organization

KNOWLEDGE IS OF TWO KINDS. WE KNOW A SUBJECT OURSELVES, OR
WE KNOW WHERE WE CAN FIND INFORMATION UPON IT.

Samuel Johnson

Over the last few years, knowledge management (KM) has begun
to gain a toehold in the world of business management, although
more from a private sector rather than a public-sector perspective. In both sectors, the KM community has begun to establish
a presence, albeit at a fairly low level, on the corporate ladder.
However, the KM community now finds itself in very much the
same role that the information management (IM) community
did in relation to the information technology (IT) community
not that long ago: that of junior business partner. This situation
has led to some inevitable entrenchment on the part of both
IT and IM communities and also to more than a little reluctance by senior managers to embrace anything new such as KM
that might distract from already established business imperatives
and directions. At the same time, many business leaders now

believe that strategically the most valuable asset of any organization is the intellectual capital of its employees and those same
senior managers unwilling to embrace KM are also being held
accountable for managing all of their corporate assets, including
knowledge.

I believe the crucial KM issue from a management perspective
is how to use knowledge to better equip employees to deliver
services more effectively and efficiently. Accordingly, more
organizations are examining the potential use of KM as a means
to help them work more effectively to meet the business challenges that confront them. Although KM holds such significant
organizational promise, there are some major obstacles that must
be overcome if it is to be implemented successfully. And the most
fundamental of these obstacles is to ensure that any KM initiative
is properly aligned with known organizational business goals and
strategies.

In 2003, a survey by KPMG of several hundred European
businesses found that more than 80 percent of senior mangers
surveyed considered knowledge to be a strategic asset in their
organizations. Yet, an equal number were unable to define what
a KM strategy should look like. So it seems there is plenty of room
for the development of KM strategies. As Michael Zack observed
in his article, "Developing a Knowledge Strategy" (*California Management Review*), many executives are unsure of how to translate the
goal of becoming a *learning organization* or a *knowing organization* into
a strategic course of action.

However an organization decides to address its KM requirements, any successful KM strategy will need to be based on
a functional business model, one that addresses the four
necessary dimensions of a KM program: people; processes;
technology; and learning. The purpose of the strategy will be
to provide a framework for the development of a decentral-
ized, flexible, and responsive KM business environment. At it
evolves, the KM strategy will need to recognize the necessary

Pillar	Dimensions	Competencies/ Key Elements
People and Leadership	Strategic planning, vision sharing, specific and general goals and objectives, executive commitment, KM programs tied to metrics, formal KM roles in existence, tangible rewards for use of KM, special recognition for knowledge sharing and performance criteria for KM items	Operational research. Management science. Psychology. Philosophy. Logic. Management information systems. Culture and Behaviour.
Organizational Processes	Operating procedures for knowledge sharing, business process reengineering (BPR), management by objectives (MBO), total quality management (TQM), metric standards, hierarchical/centralized/ decentralized, matrix-type organization, open/sharing, closed/power based, internal partnering versus competing type of culture	Operational research. Organizational development. Business language. Business rules. Best practices. Industry norms. Culture and behaviour. Philosophy. Psychology.
Technology	Data warehousing, database management, multimedia repositories, groupware, decision support systems, corporate intranet, business modeling systems, intelligent agents, neural networks, etc.	Computer science. Operational research. Engineering. Math/statistics. Logic. Management information system.
Learning	Tacit and explicit knowledge understood, sharing vision/team learning, management support for continuous learning, knowledge captured and distributed, KM values and principles formally encouraged, virtual teams/exchange forums in use, communities of practice/shared results are active, innovation encouraged/recognized/rewarded	Cognitive disciplines. Psychology. Organizational development. Systems engineering. Management philosophy. Personal mastery. Internal assessment and feedback loops. Incentives.

FIGURE 4.1 *Knowledge management (KM) strategy: planning components. Adapted from The Four Pillars of KM, George Washington University KM Model.*

interdependencies with other corporate strategies, such as those of the human resources and information technology groups, and the dimensions of knowledge and corporate competency (see Figure 4.1) that the strategy will need to plan for, coordinate, and optimize.

From a corporate perspective, it is important to realize that there are two dimensions to address as the KM strategy evolves: one is the development of the strategy itself; the other is the alignment of any KM strategy to the strategy of the organization. In other words, the KM strategy is inextricably linked to the business strategy. Sounds obvious, doesn't it? Despite it seeming to be so obvious, many KM strategies are far too monodimensional and focused on desired outcomes of organizational KM practitioners than on desired business outcomes. Unfortunately, studies show that in most companies, alignment with business strategy is neither a motivating factor nor a key evaluation criterion of KM initiatives. This invariably means that KM work becomes disconnected from the real business issues that need to be resolved and in so doing ensures that KM becomes at best a sideshow and not the main event it has the potential to be.

Remember that the goal of KM should not be self-serving. It is far more important to deal with an organization's pressing business issues and find out how KM can facilitate solving them, than it is to ensure KM is given a high profile in the organization. If you do the former well, it is likely that the latter will happen as a matter of course. So, how do you establish knowledge as a supporting capability to the business strategy? The first step is to think of knowledge alignment from two perspectives: development of a business strategy and supporting the strategy once it is developed.

In developing the business strategy—based on an approach where strategy equals organizational capabilities, knowledge plays a pivotal role in building the capabilities and organizational capacity necessary to develop further capabilities and competencies. Strategic capabilities that knowledge helps to create and maintain are typically value innovation, environmental understanding, experimentation, design capacity, predictive activity, and organizational memory. Through these types of activities, it becomes easier for an organization to identify clearly the way that knowledge enables strategy development and future maintenance.

Supporting the business strategy is a more straightforward value proposition, as knowledge plays a unique and visible role in support of desired business outcomes, especially from the standpoint of enhancing the operational infrastructure from which an organization's services and products are delivered. Particularly significant in this tactical context is knowledge used to support business performance and knowledge used to support business productivity. Knowledge-based activities in support of business performance are typically managing customer knowledge, building organizational knowledge processes, identifying knowledge and information linkages, and aggregation of organizational learning. Knowledge-based activities in support of business productivity are typically capturing and sharing best practices and other reusable knowledge assets, promotion of knowledge-based practices and processes, and coordination and management of organizational knowledge and information repositories.

The most successful KM strategies are well aligned with an overarching business strategy and tend to focus on smaller, manageable projects that help to deliver one supporting capability at a time rather than trying to address all strategic elements at once. The crucial lesson to be learned here is that there is no such thing as a supportable standalone KM strategy and that if you are the owner of such a thing you had better rethink your approach—and quickly.

The strategy that has the best hope of alignment will be one that addresses a number of fundamental business-focused questions concerning the use of knowledge in the organization:

How effective are our current knowledge practices?

Is corporate knowledge being properly optimized?

How can knowledge help make the organization more effective in the future?

Knowledge practices may often appear to be fairly mature and well supported and used, but may actually not be delivering optimal value for the organization and may not be well focused on critical performance indicators and potential future success factors or strategic objectives. The whole rationale behind deploying KM in the organization should be that it will help to achieve organizational goals, and to that end the KM strategy should exactly describe that intention.

WHERE TO BEGIN?

I cannot overstate how important it is to get a working understanding of how your organization's strategic goals and objectives are actually being implemented. Not just at the superficial level of reading mission and strategy statements, but at a far more fundamental level of how the organization actually operates in response to these strategic objectives. To do that, you need to gain an understanding of what the various functional corporate units are doing in response to those stated objectives. You need to ask those responsible for delivering business processes and products and to talk to those people throughout the organization. By discussing their business plans for the future, you will be much better placed to look at what factors might impact their reaching those objectives.

For business managers it is a simple value proposition: Is KM helping achieve their goals, and if not, how can it be better aligned with work processes in order to do so? This approach to deciding on a workable KM strategy, is really just taking the lowest common denominator in the organization, the business process, and using it as a bellwether for how KM can facilitate better business practices. If KM can be relevant at a business process level, it will ensure that any corporate strategy for KM deployment is already encompassing the necessary internal building blocks for successful alignment.

BUILD IT AND THEY WILL COME?

First, the KM strategy will need to consider three key knowledge-focused questions: Where are we now, where do we want to get to, and how do we get there? The KM strategy will be structured around the answers to these questions.

Where Are We Now?

An Analysis of the Current Situation

Are knowledge management practices and processes in place, and if so, how do they impact the organization's ability to meet its strategic objectives? How pervasive is the use of KM tools and techniques by individuals and teams in the organization? Are there inhibitors to good KM: financial, cultural, technical, or organizational? This analysis would typically take the shape of a knowledge audit or survey. The audit is aimed at garnering an understanding of what knowledge needs the organization has, what knowledge assets or resources it has and where they are, what gaps exist in its knowledge processes and practices, and to what extent its people, processes, and technology currently support or hamper the effective management of knowledge. This is basically a SWOT (strengths, weaknesses, opportunities and threats) exercise, and the results will help the organization plan future KM activity in response to what is revealed. However, remember there is a cautionary tale (see Chapter 7, "Lessons Learned") about KM surveys, so get a feel for the true scope of this one first before getting in too deep.

Where Do We Want to Get?

This is essentially an overview of what KM will do for the organization in response to the business issues and gaps highlighted by the audit/survey analysis. This is where you have an opportunity to describe how the organization will look when good KM practices are in place and specifically to tell how KM will help individuals and teams to work more effectively together. It is also a good opportunity to outline some realistic measurements that will help gauge progress, and allow the organization to evaluate the return on its KM investment.

How Do We Get There?

Here's where the master plan will get addressed, showing the specific actions that will need to be undertaken. This action plan needs to include the four essential focus areas of KM: people, process, technology, and training.

How will you engage people in taking on KM accountabilities and responsibilities?

How will you embed KM techniques into business processes?

What tools will you deploy to facilitate better KM practices and how will the corporate technology infrastructure support them?

What awareness and training programs are you proposing?

Assessment of the preceding needs must include details of human and financial resources requirements, deliverables, likely timescales, and responsibilities. Above all, the strategy needs to be flexible enough to leave some "wiggle" room for any hidden issues that may impact it downstream, such as a change in senior management focus and commitment or even strategic direction.

WHERE'S THE BEEF?

Once the overarching components for the strategy are in place, it is necessary to start building the tactical development and implementation components that will deliver on the strategy and ensure its proper alignment with the organization's business objectives. Here are some areas of focus that will need to be considered:

What's the Case for Knowledge Management in the Organization?

Has anyone made a compelling case for KM? Probably not, although I expect you will be able to find an organizational definition of knowledge management somewhere, but even if there is such a definition, it is still likely that someone needs to take the time to explain to people how KM connects to real day-to-day business issues. The role of the KM evangelist is one that is necessary in all organizations. The critical factor here is that any evangelizing needs to be firmly grounded in supporting evidence showing how KM will help the organization achieve its business goals. This is the place for a KM vision and definition (if you need one) and some high-level objectives, but remember if it is not practical, it is not tactical.

Who Are the Stakeholders, and What Challenges and Knowledge Needs do They Have?

To succeed with any KM strategy, it is crucial that people in the organization can see their business issues reflected in the strategy. This does not mean you are going to be able to summarize all the business challenges and requirements of every employee in great detail, but it does mean you will need to have talked with all levels in the organization to get a flavor of the issues they face. The stakeholder community will include senior and middle mangers, as well as line managers, business process owners and knowledge workers, so this initial scoping activity is a significant one, not just in terms of time commitments, but also in terms of long-term impact for KM in the organization.

The Strategy and Associated Action Plan Details

This is where the business owners need to be engaged, even if they are not too excited by the prospect. Clarity and practicality are absolutely paramount at this stage if you want to bring the business onside with your plans. In this case, less is a virtue, as long as it is clearly laid out and, above all, appears to be doable. Do everything possible to demystify the whole plan, and always use business, not KM, terminology. Place deliverables and activities into specific domains or themes that are easily understandable by everyone (e.g., KM planning and decision processes, KM business processes, KM tools and techniques, KM policies and guidelines, KM skills development, KM communications, KM governance, etc.). Everyone should be able to clearly see who owns and promotes the strategy, how it will be promoted, how it will be developed and implemented (and when), and how it will be evaluated and measured. In essence, a simple outline of what needs to happen and when it needs to happen to move forward and translate the strategy into action.

Dependencies and Risks

Here is where you can build some latitude into the plan. Take the time to consider what dependencies already exist, such as senior management approval of budgets or the availability of personnel, but also take the opportunity to create the case for inter-dependencies with other corporate areas such as IT and human resources (HR). The reason? If you can create an understanding of how KM activity will further other group's agendas, you stand a far better chance of succeeding. The old adage about there being safety in numbers holds true, especially when it comes down to decisions that are likely to be made at the senior manager's table. KM can definitely be seen as an enabling function from an HR perspective. After all, most HR groups are promoting self-management of career and the need for better retention and recruitment planning for key corporate knowledge personnel. KM certainly facilitates that agenda. Similarly, KM can be positioned as a possible missing link from the corporate IT group's perspective. After all, IT groups have spent deeply on installing a technology infrastructure, but where is the true payback to the organization? It could be argued that the real payback comes when technology systems are used to capture, share, and reuse corporate knowledge assets to make the business more effective. The beauty of this position is that KM is a nonthreatening entity from an IT perspective. KM does not place any additional demands on the IT group—it makes IT's position even stronger as a support function that enables the business to operate in a more effective manner.

When it comes to risks, you should always spell out the impact of actually doing nothing. The status quo may have its supporters, but if its feasible then at least try to engage them in a conversation about KM, rather than just have them take an opposing stance behind your back. You may not win the argument, but at least you will be forewarned of the internal issues and likely obstacles that may lie in your way.

Highlight risks that allow for synergies with the other corporate areas already mentioned. For example, most organizations are going to be affected by the boomer-boomer drain or a high attrition rate due to other factors. Either way, this is a risk that is easily understood by all business managers and can be useful as a means to start alliances with other groups that will have account-ability for managing that risk. Always look to find synergy and prospective partnering opportunities whenever you can, as KM will need all the friends it can get if you want to try and change the way that business is done.

WORTH CONSIDERING

Before getting too deeply into the work plan, it is probably worth taking some time to think through what corporate posi-tions and messages you want to convey. By this I mean that most business units will want to craft their own approach to their KM issues, but usually feel comfortable operating within known organizational parameters, or at least on the edges of them. Therefore, some guidance is likely to be needed to help encourage common approaches to be adopted. In some cases, this may take the form of policy, but given the usual response of business units to policy imperatives (i.e., pay it lip service and avoid its more severe limitations wherever possible), it will probably be better to produce a set of principles for KM or high-level guidelines. This approach leaves an impression of discretionary rather than mandatory approach to KM decision-making for the organization, and tends to get more accomplished in the long run. The following are some questions its worth thinking about before attempting to produce any such guiding principles:

Is the primary KM focus for the organization to be on its people, its processes or its technology or will you try and address all three together, or maybe a combination of them?
Is the focus for managing knowledge going to be mainly external, (e.g., customers and customer relationships,

market forces, competition, etc.), internal, (e.g., capturing knowledge, roles and responsibilities, business processes, community evolution, etc.), or a combination of both?

Is the focus for capturing knowledge to be on explicit (e.g., connecting people with information) or tacit (e.g., connecting people with people) knowledge, or a combination of both?

Is the focus for exploiting knowledge capital to be on what's already there (e.g., data search and manipulation) or will it be on facilitating and capturing new knowledge and innovation?

Is the focus for making knowledge visible to be on the mapping of subject expertise (e.g., expert networks and directories) or will it be on the support mechanisms for communities of practice or interest?

Is the focus for intensifying corporate knowledge to be based on gathering product knowledge (e.g., help desks), gathering customer knowledge (e.g., customer service teams) or gathering organizational knowledge (e.g., expert communities)?

Whatever you decide, you will need to set some corporate priorities for those wanting to move the KM yardsticks forward (e.g., communities are the prime corporate focus, then customer relationships, or whatever.) The reason for this is that no matter how well intentioned and even well resourced the KM initiative may be, it is simply impossible to do it all at once. Many business unit initiatives fail for this very reason, and to be truthful, the narrower the focus the better, at least initially. Remember that you are looking to build momentum through a series of manageable and doable projects, not attempting to change the organization overnight. I would strongly recommend using a pilot project as a test environment before launching any new knowledge management initiative. By using this approach you will be able to see exactly what works, or more importantly doesn't work, before getting in too deep. You can also refine your approach based on what you learn, and it will provide you a solid platform for future progress. The fact that you can point to a real-life example to show that what you are advocating actually works in practice, is a very powerful tool. Also it is worth noting that working in such a contained environment, means that any problems you encountered along the way should not have created any negative impressions of KM in the minds of the organization as a whole.

GETTING GOING

Now you have some sense of what will resonate with the business units, it is time to target some KM initiatives that you believe have a reasonable chance of providing a successful outcome. These *quick wins* are often referred to as the *low-hanging fruit*, the ones most easily picked. It does not necessarily have to be in an area of core competence for the organization, but if you can find a partnering opportunity with such a competency area, it will help align KM with real-time business issues quicker than almost anything else. However, the real trick is to provide a winning combination of quick wins along with something substantive that can be viewed as building corporate KM capacity for the future. Whatever you decide to focus on, try and pick a few core activities where you think you can make a difference, and go with those.

Quick Wins

A good place to start looking for a quick win is in area where communities naturally evolve, and where work processes tend to be supportive in nature. A good example of such a business discipline would be project or program management. Although to be truthful, any expert community is a likely breeding ground for KM activity, especially as they tend to have the right mindset for community participation and the sharing and reuse of knowledge. However, I would personally start with project management, and for that there are a number of reasons:

Project management is structured around the management and measurement of multiple project activities, and that allows for additional threads, such as KM, to be easily included as just one more task that needs to be managed. In other words, to some extent KM can be hidden among the pack, and while KM is not likely to be seen as a critical path activity, it can both help facilitate other tasks, as well as be a beneficiary of the outcomes of those tasks.

As the project evolves, the interdependencies between KM and the other project activities will become clear. This evolution of dependency can have a positive effect on how KM is perceived and valued within the organization.

Project managers are by definition individuals who perceive the value of collaborative approaches to problem solving and who encourage the capture, sharing, and reuse of knowledge. In fact, most projects already have the foundation pieces of a robust KM infrastructure already in place through the use of techniques such as project reviews, the capture of lessons learned and best practices, and the use of repositories to store project documentation.

Once the project is delivered, the benefits of KM as a business-enabling activity can be properly promoted. The ripple effect of good publicity, starting with the project community, can soon spread across the organization and help position KM in a positive light.

Corporate Capacity

This is where you can start building for the future. The KM infrastructure you are putting in place will need to include some high-level building blocks: maybe a KM policy, probably some KM guiding principles, and a plan for raising corporate KM awareness and competency levels.

A KM policy is a difficult one to position in the organization: Should it be sponsored by a central group such as the chief information officer (CIO) sector or the administration group or should it be sponsored through a business unit? My preference would be for a business sponsor, although most of the policies I have seen seem to have come through one of the central groups. The danger with a central-produced policy is that it may suffer the fate that most other corporate policies seem to suffer: A degree of lip-service may be paid to it, but little if any practical application is given to it. This is why I endorse having a business unit sponsor the policy—because it will need to be seen as a practical business tool, one that can be applied to daily business processes. Any policy you create will need to involve stakeholders throughout the organization, support the creation and maintenance of communities, validate the stewardship of knowledge, promote the maintenance and use of knowledge as a corporate asset, and, encourage open and collaborative work habits.

Guiding principles for KM may be an easier sell in the organization. This does not mean it has to be an either/or situation between KM principles and a KM policy: Both can happily coexist, but you may decide it makes more sense to focus on the promotion of only one, especially if you are starting from ground zero in terms of organizational KM awareness. Any principles you produce will need to guide the organization in consistently planning and evaluating its options and rendering its business decisions. Principles should also be able to stand the test of time and be able to accommodate the evolution in business objectives, technologies, processes, standards, and products that occurs in any organization. The following are areas you should focus on:

Accountability: Every employee is accountable to manage knowledge as a corporate asset.

Planning and coordination: Business planning, budget planning, service delivery planning and day-to-day operational planning should consider the management of knowledge assets throughout their life cycle (capture, access, sharing, retention, disposal).

Communication: Each employee, whether individually or as a member of a community or work team, should be accountable to share and reuse knowledge with others in the organization.

Infrastructure: Information systems should be designed and implemented to help the sharing of knowledge.

Accessibility: Knowledge should be made accessible throughout the organization so it can be reused many times.

Value: KM decisions and investments should be done in a context that supports the strategic business objectives of the organization.

Quality assurance: KM initiatives should consider content management practices (i.e., ease of use, accountability, stewardship, reliability, quality, timeliness, preservation, etc.) and ensure quality control procedures are in place.

Horizontality: Any standards for KM should complement other corporate and industry standards and accepted best practices, and be used to ensure common approaches and methods are applied to business problems across the organization.

KM awareness and competency: This component addresses two requirements: the need to raise corporate and individual awareness around the subject of KM and the need to provide individuals with the skills necessary to meet the objectives for managing knowledge in the organization.

These are crucial foundation pieces that you need to put in place if you want to help align KM with the business.

Awareness: There are a number of communications objectives that you are targeting here including the following:

- Developing a clear and common organizational grasp of the language and purpose of KM.
- Raising the awareness of KM's significance to employees and clientele.
- Eliciting support from employees and motivating them to share their knowledge.
- Promoting KM objectives, benefits, and scope to employees and encouraging middle managers to consider implementing KM initiatives.
- Helping employees gain an understanding of any existing organizational knowledge community.

At the same time as raising awareness about KM, it is also a good idea to provide people with something tangible that they can reference regarding KM—for example, a KM brochure designed to spread awareness regarding what KM is, why it is important, and how it affects people at the individual level. A particularly powerful tool to use is something called a *knowledge charter*. This is a document stating the intent of the organization to manage its knowledge in a diligent and focused manner and should be signed by the senior management, preferably in some public place where many employees are gathered. The ideal setup is to have the senior manager talk about managing corporate knowledge and then have him or her sign the charter, followed by the senior managers. The charter is purely symbolic, but carries a strong message that the organization takes KM seriously.

You can also look for opportunities to raise awareness and foster partnerships through briefings and presentations to business teams and expert communities. The use of ongoing information sessions to regularly inform interested employees of internal KM-based work and projects is also a powerful tool. If you are ready for it, you might also consider hosting a *knowledge day* for the organization. If successful, this can become an annual event, one where you can use internal and external examples and case studies to promote and praise the application of KM in the business.

Finally, do not forget to look to the stakeholder community for feedback about the awareness program. Remember, you are looking for alignment with the business drivers of the organization and if your audience does not see that objective being fulfilled, you will need to adjust your program accordingly.

Competency

This is an opportunity to team with others in the organization, the HR group for example, to target areas where KM competencies are required such as front-line officers, program officers, communications and policy officials, and so forth to improve operational levels. This might involve setting up a formal training infrastructure or perhaps some informal knowledge-exchange sessions. Much depends on how seriously your organization is addressing KM and how willing employees are to devote time to it. The feedback you receive from the awareness program should give a fair indication of which route to take, at least to begin with. My personal preference is always to start with something small along the lines of the informal sessions and then to try to build demand for a more formal program that way.

Anyway, whichever path you choose to follow, here are some areas to consider:

The inclusion of KM components in the orientation session for new employees.

A knowledge-sharing mentorship program for employees seeking to become managers.

KM training modules each focusing on a different theme—for example, a KM 101 module or a KM best-practices module, and so forth.

Knowledge-transfer guidelines designed to encourage the retention of knowledge assets when employees leave their positions.

Depending on how successful the competency program is, you might want to consider measuring its impact on the organization. This needs to be considered carefully, as you want to measure something quantifiable (e.g., numbers of employees who have received KM training) rather than something qualitative (e.g., whether the organization's culture has changed). Stick to hard numeric measures is my advice because they are hard to argue with, whereas quality is a subjective matter and can be a weakness for any program as it is less easy to define and defend.

The bottom line is that you are looking to achieve a minimum level of KM competency in every new employee and as many of the current workforce as can be realistically achieved.

THE FAMOUS "ME" QUESTION

Remember that to gain acceptance and support for your KM strategy you must answer the question that is most fundamental to your employees: What's in it for me? If you want to get aligned with the organization, you need to be able to answer this question from the perspective of the individual, the team, the managers, the senior managers, and any possible permutation of these groups. To do so you must to point to demonstrable outcomes, not just repeat apocryphal evidence ad nauseam. This is where the timing of any KM initiatives will be important, and if you have any internal success stories ready, especially from any KM pilot projects, here is where you are going to promote them to greatest effect. Particularly effective is to have the business managers who have actually benefited from any KM work become the spokespersons for your KM endeavors. Among the benefits to employees that you may want to focus on are increased knowledge awareness, creation, and innovation opportunities; improvements in services and products through better knowledge-based processes; availability of expertise through better knowledge-sharing practices; and improvement in problem-solving capacity for individuals.

Above all, remember to adhere to real-life examples from your own organization whenever possible.

ANYTHING ELSE?

If we cannot devise practical ways to tie KM to the desired business outcome of having employees better equipped to deliver services and products it will never advance as a business discipline. Only when we have shown tangible evidence of the enabling capabilities of KM can we hope to get a meaningful dialogue under way between business units and the KM community. This does not mean you cannot start KM initiatives before the dialogue is under way, but you do need to be realistic about what you can achieve without it. In fact you may find the organization is taking on KM initiatives before any actual KM strategy is in place. This is not necessarily a bad thing, as I mentioned earlier it may be more effective to dry run a few KM pilots in the business units before you engage the wider organization anyway.

A winning strategy for any KM initiative needs to address many different organizational requirements—fiscal, cultural, and operational—and yet it also has to have the virtue of simplicity. Any plan for KM must set realistic, yet attainable, goals and should resonate well with any organizational audience at any level. Most of all it needs to be aligned properly with the over-arching business goals and strategies of the organization. Make it real to your employees by using their own business language, and if you can make it sound interesting then so much the better.

In the end, if people can see clear benefits to participation in KM activity and understand what you are trying to do with those activities, your KM strategy stands a good chance of achieving alignment with the organization as a whole, and also stands a good chance of being a success.

TAKE-AWAY MENU

Here are five things worth remembering about aligning KM:

1. Start developing any KM strategy by first gaining a thorough understanding of the organization's business strategies and goals.
2. Make sure you have mapped out and fully understood the interdependencies between your KM strategy and other corporate strategies such as HR or IT.
3. Find where knowledge can play a supporting role in the development of corporate capabilities and competencies and use that value proposition as the context for your alignment strategy.
4. Find where knowledge can help make the organization more effective in the future and link those areas to the organization's long-term goals in your KM strategy.
5. Go deep and talk with the organization's business owners and operators to see how KM can align with their business plans and desired outcomes, and use that alignment as a momentum-builder for your KM strategy.

FIVE

Deploying Knowledge Management in the Organization

IF YOU WANT TO MAKE ENEMIES, TRY AND CHANGE SOMETHING.

Woodrow Wilson

Now that the marketing campaign is under way, and the strategy for knowledge management (KM) is closely aligned with the overall business strategy, it is time to start planning for the actual deployment of KM in the organization.

The first major obstacle in your way is that most business managers are skeptical about making the necessary investment in KM. They will tell you that time is too short, resources are too scarce, and there is no appetite for radical change. Yet, public servants are inundated with legal accountabilities that tell them they have to manage all resources, including knowledge and information, better. For instance, the Canadian government is overloaded with legislation that establishes employee responsibilities in the areas of KM and information management (IM), over 30 acts,

policies, and charters in all. The same now holds true in the private sector with a variety of legal obligations like Sarbanes-Oxley imposing ever more complexity into an already overloaded work environment. Try making sense of all those myriad accountabilities and responsibilities in your daily work processes, many of which were designed long before legislative imperatives came marching over the horizon. The problem with any legislation is that it only tells half of the story, it describes the desired conclusion quite nicely, but does nothing to help with developing the characters and plot necessary to reach the desired happy ending. It is self-evident that many work processes will need some fine-tuning to ensure they can accommodate all these new legislative requirements. Responding to these kinds of challenges is where KM can show its true value, and in so doing can win the confidence of business managers keen to find better and more effective ways of doing business.

To help with deployment of KM in the organization, you can use a basic template of high-level actions needed to guide activity and priorities in a staged and logical flow, and to help to plan and manage workload and expectation levels. This is often referred to as a *roadmap*. Although I believe it is important to use a roadmap, I'd suggest that the optimal way to do so is to leave plenty of wiggle room for unexpected detours, roadwork, or traffic jams along the way. In other words, use it to your advantage but do not close your mind to others taking the journey in different directions than you had planned for. The roadmap we used at PWGSC was developed by the Canadian Institute of Knowledge Management (CIKM) and is shown in Figure 5-1. It proved an essential planning tool for the KM Office and was most effective in explaining our activities to senior managers and in helping to establish a level of understanding and alignment with the other knowledge community stakeholders in the department.

On the basis of the roadmap activities, we were able to look at managing and measuring KM maturity in the organization and

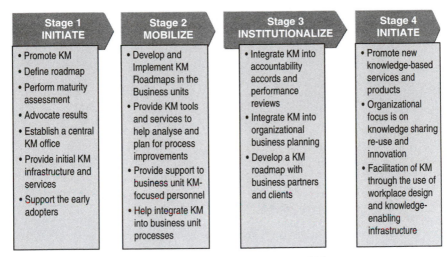

Stage 1 INITIATE	Stage 2 MOBILIZE	Stage 3 INSTITUTIONALIZE	Stage 4 INITIATE
• Promote KM • Define roadmap • Perform maturity assessment • Advocate results • Establish a central KM office • Provide initial KM infrastructure and services • Support the early adopters	• Develop and Implement KM Roadmaps in the Business units • Provide KM tools and services to help analyse and plan for process improvements • Provide support to business unit KM-focused personnel • Help integrate KM into business unit processes	• Integrate KM into accountability accords and performance reviews • Integrate KM into organizational business planning • Develop a KM roadmap with business partners and clients	• Promote new knowledge-based services and products • Organizational focus is on knowledge sharing re-use and innovation • Facilitation of KM through the use of workplace design and knowledge-enabling infrastructure

(Adapted from the Enterprise KM Roadmap, CIKM – Dr. Randy Frid)

FIGURE 5.1   *Deployment activity.*

to lay a foundation for the renewal of business processes from a knowledge-based perspective in business units. To do so, you will need to begin by partnering with business units to evaluate their business processes and to start the planning and decision-making processes necessary to convert KM principles into practices. At Public Works and Government Services Canada (PWGSC), we found that within any specific business unit, KM works on discrete business processes in much the same way and that a basic set of KM management and measurement activities are needed. We worked with the CIKM to produce a checklist of process improvement criteria, including the following:

- What do people know?
- What people do not know?
- How to best leverage people's knowledge?
- How to convince people to share knowledge?
- How to map what people know to a business process?
- How to fill knowledge gaps?

- How to capture unique knowledge?
- How to prevent knowledge loss unless such a loss is *planned abandonment*?
- To whom or what to turn when people need to fill a knowledge gap?
- How to get people the knowledge they need, when they need it?
- How to repair knowledge processes if they fail?
- How to institutionalize successful knowledge processes?
- How to capture and advocate lessons learned and best practices?
- How to value unique and proprietary corporate knowledge?

Once under way, you should try to persuade the various business units to adopt common KM guidelines, procedures, and methodologies to maximize the return on the huge intellectual assets that they hold on behalf of their organization. Underpinning all of that should be a set of management principles that bind KM to business goals.

The likelihood is that most of the business units you will deal with will be in a state of flux, with changes of personnel, as well as business pressures and changing objectives, impacting them on a regular basis. Given that likely background, the key to success will be in proceeding at a manageable pace. Change fatigue is a potential problem and must be factored in to any KM plan. Without some degree of stability in the organization, it is almost impossible to get anyone's attention for long enough to start showing how KM can help them work better and more effectively. Accordingly, you would be well served to start by looking at the organizational structure of the business units involved and analyzing where the main points of stability are. For example, a long-term employee who has worked on the help desk for many years is probably a better bet to start a KM conversation with than a team leader who is moving fast up the corporate ladder. Continuity is the name of the game here, and as KM is a non-hierarchical activity it can just as easily produce good results at any point in the business process you wish to apply it.

What does a winning deployment strategy for a KM initiative look like? Is it a clear directive from the head of the organization—"thou shalt, because I am telling you to"—in other words a top-down approach. Or is it a grassroots kind of an initiative—"I think I will, because I believe it is a good idea to"—in other words a bottom-up approach where individuals decide for themselves. Actually both approaches have a certain appeal and both can be effective depending on the individual circumstances of the organization. It is possible to achieve a happy combination of the two approaches, but typically the grassroots one is the one that is likely to survive, especially if the original senior champion moves on or the senior leadership decides to focus the organization elsewhere. Personally, my belief is that there is only one way to succeed and that is to just do it without worrying too much about the necessary inspirational leadership quotient. It is really what stealth KM is all about.

Whichever deployment approach you decide to go with, there are a number of crucial steps in the process that you need to consider and address. These involve both the management of the structure of the central KM group as well as the management of the wider business community. These steps are needed whether you are dealing with an individual business unit or the organization as a whole.

Step One: Ask Crucial Questions

If we want to help people to get comfortable with KM as a business management tool that can help them meet their organizational objectives and legislative obligations, there are three crucial questions we will need to be able to address on their behalf:

How is KM relevant to what I do?
What specifically am I expected to do?
What's in it for me?

If we do not have answers to all these questions, and especially the last one, then we have little, if any, hope of transforming our business processes. Because, to change an organization's view of KM, you have to first get people onside with the concepts of KM. Once onside, they can help change your culture by changing the business processes that embody it.

Relevance of Knowledge Management

KM is generally neither well understood nor properly valued by the leaders of most organizations. We need to do a much better job of demystifying these two disciplines and find a way to show that they are neither elitist nor impractical. The surest route to that desired outcome is to connect at a practical level with business units and business managers. If you cannot use KM tools and techniques to improve business processes, I think the answer to the original question is that KM is not very relevant to the business. However, once you have worked with any business group to improve a business process, then KM is relevant, and you can prove it.

What Is Expected from Employees?

You will need to set a basic level of expectation for all employees without overloading an already busy work environment.

At a minimum, every employee should receive some education about the concepts of KM and what you are targeting for KM deployment within the organization. An ideal way to achieve this level of basic education is to work with the HR group to include a KM module in the employee orientation session. Orientation sessions typically run for a half or a full day, and you should easily be able to cover off the basic concepts in a 30-minute overview. Employees need to be told that they are responsible for managing the organization's knowledge, as they would any other corporate asset. The knowledge management steps of capturing, sharing, and reusing knowledge can be emphasized, and the technology tools available to facilitate this management (e.g., portals, collaboration software, etc.) can be alluded to. In this way, every employee will gain some familiarity with KM as a corporate business management process.

What Is the Intended Payback?

The second part of the orientation describes what the employee, and thereby the organization, will receive by way of payback for doing KM. Here is where you can outline a more effective decision-making capacity for the individual and the organization. You may not want to get into too much detail, as every individual is likely to see KM from his or her own perspective and is equally likely to see the payback in terms of themselves as individuals. Stick with the big-picture view, because the bottom line is that KM is about making better decisions together, nothing more. You can also draw the connection to senior management's accountability to manage corporate knowledge as a valued business asset and remind your audience that many experts are now saying that a business's intellectual capital is likely to be its most valuable corporate asset.

Both the expectations and payback guidance can be cranked up a notch when you are working with business units directly, as you will then need to be far more specific in describing actual roles and responsibilities for managing knowledge.

Remember that this step is as much about asking for other's input, as it is for you to impart knowledge to the organization. Also always keep an open mind and never assume that you already know how KM will be relevant to any individual or business group. One of the joys of KM being so broad and deep in scope is that you are always being surprised as to how others see its relevance to their business issues and how they view its potential benefits to them as individuals and teams.

STEP TWO: CREATE A SET OF GUIDING PRINCIPLES FOR MANAGING KNOWLEDGE

To achieve some sort of consistency of approaches to KM work in the organization, you should work with a representative focus group to decide on some guiding principles for knowledge-based work in the organization. Principles are corporate-level statements highlighting the fundamental values of an organization and should help guide the organization in consistently planning and evaluating its options and rendering its business decisions. They also need to highlight the fundamental values of the organization and be able to stand the test of time and accommodate any evolution in business objectives, technologies, processes, standards, and products that may occur. The principles can help with commonality and consistency of approaches and serve as a reference point for project teams, expert communities, and individuals.

The ideal situation is to have them reviewed and endorsed by a senior governance committee, preferably one with responsibility for business issues. Once you have some buyin you can promote these principles with the intention that anyone can adopt and implement them. Even if people decide to customize them to better reflect their own business issues, you will at the very least have advanced the KM agenda and got people considering how best to manage their own knowledge assets.

The following are eight guiding principles you may wish to consider to get started:

1. Accountability: Every employee is accountable to manage knowledge as corporate asset, in accordance with government and organizational legislation and/or policies. Knowledge assets are to be managed with the same rigor as other organizational assets (human resources, financial, physical) to ensure corporate knowledge is leveraged to provide maximum benefit to the organization's employees and clients.

2. Planning and coordination: Business planning, budget planning, service delivery planning and day-to-day operational planning should consider the management of knowledge assets throughout their life cycle (capture, access, sharing, retention, disposal). Partnering approaches between stakeholders are encouraged.

3. Collaboration and knowledge exchange: Each employee, whether individually or as a member of a community or work team, will be encouraged to collaborate with others in the organization and be accountable to share and reuse knowledge with others to help improve organizational effectiveness and service quality to clients.

4. Infrastructure: Electronic systems are the preferred means of creating, storing, using, and managing knowledge assets. Investments in these systems shall consider corporate information technology (IT) architectures (existing and planned technologies) to maximize value. Electronic systems should be designed and implemented

to easily locate and retrieve information, and to facilitate sharing of information and knowledge across the organization, subject to legal constraints.

5.   Accessibility: Corporate knowledge will be made accessible throughout the organization based on demonstrated user needs. There should be single authoritative virtual repositories for knowledge assets (i.e., knowledge will be captured once and reused many times).

6.   Value: Knowledge management decisions and investments will be done in a corporate context (supports strategic business objectives of the organization), be approved by the appropriate governance committee for KM, and be rendered using value management techniques that foster consolidation and coordination of business needs. KM initiatives must promote or enhance effectiveness, efficiency, economies, and functional capabilities for the organization and be developed and maintained using performance measurement assessment techniques.

7.   Quality assurance: KM initiatives will consider content management practices (i.e., ease of use, accountability, stewardship, reliability, quality, timeliness, preservation) and ensure quality control procedures are in place.

8.   Horizontality: Corporate guidance for KM will complement industry standards and accepted best practices to ensure common approaches and methods are applied to business problems across the organization.

STEP THREE: FIND PRACTICAL WAYS TO MOVE FORWARD

You also need to find ways of moving your KM principles forward. To address the questions of fit and relevance, you may wish to consider conducting a KM maturity survey or audit, aimed at assessing the state of the organization's KM practices and skills. You may want to focus on a single business unit to assess the state of affairs, as surveying the whole organization is time-consuming and has many attendant risks (as described in Chapter 7, "Lessons Learned"). No matter what level you begin with, the data you gather will be useful in gaining an understanding of the operation, assessing the gaps and impacts, and starting to plan ways of addressing areas of concern.

Whatever you discover by way of issues, you will want to focus much of your initial efforts on tactical areas where KM has not had any real impact yet, such as processes and practices. Look to find business units willing to partner with you on knowledge enabling their processes. Try to target a group that has a core corporate competency area, such as project management or asset management, to begin with. Even if you focus on a single process, you can have a major impact on the organization's perception about KM, if you can demonstrate a measurable improvement in either efficiency, or delivery quality, or both.

Above all, look to leverage what has already been done in the organization, and especially where IT is concerned, where investment has already been made. Plan to make use of infrastructure investment to start addressing some of the knowledge challenges you face. For example, most organizations will already have spent considerable time and money in building IT/IM capacity on such things as enterprise document and records management systems. You can probably use an existing records and document management system to start capturing knowledge profiles as documents are created and stored. This is the first step towards establishing a knowledge directory, or map, for the organization, one that shows who has the knowledge, where they are, and what their work portfolio looks like. Once captured in a repository tool, the directory can be navigated by any individual looking for expert knowledge and can also be used by human resources (HR) and business managers to start planning retention and replacement strategies for key knowledge workers and their areas of subject expertise.

Also remember that every organization is likely to have an e-mail system, and you might be pleasantly surprised at how much functionality is available, and unused, in the average e-mail system. For example, coordinating and categorizing e-mail content, as well as allowing users to share calendar, tasks, contacts, notes, and journal folders. While e-mail products may not be as functionally rich as a specialized collaboration tool, you can still support a knowledge community, at least at a basic level, through the average e-mail application.

If nothing else, these kinds of approaches to leveraging existing technologies are a very direct rebuttal to managers who insist that doing KM means a huge new level of investment for the organization in terms of new technologies and tools.

Whatever you do, the key principles here are to keep it simple, keep it practical, and integrate into existing workflows and work processes wherever possible.

STEP FOUR: DEVELOP SOME SUPPORTING TOOLS AND PROCESSES

To facilitate the work of knowledge workers and communities, you should consider what tools and processes can help support them in their daily work. What do employees need to help with KM analysis, planning, decision making, and connecting to organizational knowledge and expertise? The deployment of collaboration software is an obvious place to start with. Unfortunately it is no longer a simple environment, as collaboration tools now encompass instant messaging, Web-based learning tools, workgroup software, project management software, portals, self-service applications, virtual-learning classrooms, traditional KM systems, and many others. What this all means is that there is a significant danger of IT anarchy developing if collaboration is not put into a wider organizational context. To prevent a state of anarchy developing, it is necessary to develop a long-term strategy for collaboration practices in the organization, one that emphasizes collaborative approaches from the perspective of process performance and improvement. An emphasis on business processes should help to focus individuals and teams on collaborative approaches that will have the broadest reach in the organization and the most business focus. The ideal approach is to combine operational efficiencies (through integrating collaboration capacity with normal business processes) with a central and planned collaboration strategy. Easier said then done I will admit, but without some blueprint for collaboration being in place, individuals and business units will be happy enough to chart their own course, and you will soon find yourself with even more knowledge silos to contend with.

Another crucial area of focus is that of business processes from a KM perspective. An understanding of how knowledge flows within processes is vital to a proper appreciation of the inputs, linkages, and dependencies that form the basis for quality service. It is here that you will gain traction for KM in any business, and it is here that you would be well served to think of producing some early guidelines or templates that business units can use to determine how KM can help improve their processes. The intention is to help them to locate any disconnected processes, and see if it is possible to fix them through the application of KM tools and techniques. In other words, creating a context where the relationship between intellectual capital and adding business value through knowledge can be articulated by business units.

The creation and application of individual knowledge in business processes is a key component in recognizing and supporting the competencies necessary to deliver superior services or products. It is this marriage of the human and systematic elements of

a process that you will need to focus on with business units willing to explore the benefits of applying KM techniques. Typical
processes where this knowledge-based approach is easily applied
might be sales analysis and trending, customer relationship management, client services, and so forth. In fact, any process where
current knowledge combines with previous knowledge to inform
and guide the next step in the process.

Work on producing a basic methodology or template for how
business units can integrate KM into their business processes.
Here is a five-step methodology that can be applied in any
business area:

1.   Process selection: Look at the core processes only, and do
     not get sidetracked into trying to fix everything at once.
     The reason for this is that, like it or not, business man-
     agers are really only interested in a bare minimum of the
     processes they manage: those that are problematic, have
     high-visibility, or are seen as being crucial to success. If
     you fix processes that are not in any of these categories,
     you may have a successful outcome, but if no one is inter-
     ested, or sees a value, in it then you are wasting everyone's
     time.

2.   Process redesign: Embedding knowledge into business
     processes requires a process analysis and design stage to
     be completed first. It is important to involve all stake-
     holders at this stage, and this would typically include IT,
     business owners and customers, and knowledge analysts.
     Many business process redesign methodologies are avail-
     able for use, but whichever methodology gets applied it is
     most important that the process analysis reflects the true
     complexity of the work environment. The analysis needs
     to identify ways in which knowledge can enhance the pro-
     cess and ways in which technology can help to facilitate
     access to knowledge and help integrate it into the process.

3. Knowledge analysis and design: Understanding where people need information to do their job and where knowledge can be best applied to facilitate that requirement is what this step is all about. To begin, you will need to assess the needs of the process' users and decide where there may be disconnects between actual knowledge expectations and the meeting of those expectations. Once gaps have been identified, you can begin to look for ways to better organize the knowledge flows and delivery mechanisms. Remember to incorporate existing best practices, tacit learning, and existing knowledge into a more coherent set of linkages. Look for the subject experts that hold crucial knowledge and incorporate their knowledge input into any interactions between the structured and less-structured aspects of the process.

4. Knowledge context: It is most important to provide the organizational context for any knowledge, as this will have a significant impact on the ways that people understand and use it. The context you provide the knowledge becomes its brand and will help make it visible and accessible to all. It also helps to build an organizational view to knowledge relating to best practices, topics, lessons learned, subject expertise, and business intelligence. This contextualizing exercise can provide important inputs to further process improvements and helps supply knowledge that may find a broader application in the organization.

5. Knowledge value management: As the value proposition for embedding knowledge components into your business processes was to improve them, you will need to find a way to measure that improvement. You do not need to look at this from a KM perspective as such. You would probably be better off using a standard business measure such as accuracy, reliability, timeliness, or client

satisfaction to show improvement. In this way, you can measure value added as viewed through a business lens and that will help you in terms of KM's visibility and credibility with the business community. Finally, you should put in place some review mechanisms to ensure that you can take corrective measures, if necessary, to ensure that the knowledge components in the process remain fresh, relevant and timely.

STEP FIVE: SET REALISTIC EXPECTATIONS

One of the most fundamental issues to be faced is that of setting a realistic expectation level within the organization for the impact that KM will have on the business. It is vital that everyone understands that KM is not a silver bullet and that it is just another business management discipline that succeeds or fails dependent on how relevant it is to the business and how much attention they are prepared to give to it. The message is simple: KM is about using knowledge to make better decisions together, nothing more.

At the same time, it is important to start addressing the issue of change management, the people factor. With the arrival of the Intranet, change management became inextricably linked with KM in the eyes of many. Some organizations thought that the advent of technology-based opportunities for sharing and collaboration would automatically propel their organizations toward becoming knowledge-based entities. They thought that everyone in the organization would be motivated to share information and a new operating model would naturally evolve. Unfortunately, that has not been the case and the need for a more traditional change management approach is still as important as ever, one that is focused on both individual and organizational learning as a means to improve the quality of business practices and processes.

While the culture of the organization is a crucial factor in the chances of KM being successful, it is also evident that cultures are infinitely adaptable given the right set of circumstances. I believe that it is the other *C-word*—communications—that we should be more concerned with. Current KM survey data highlights lack of communications as the single biggest reason that KM initiatives fail. In their book, *Unlocking Knowledge Assets*, Susan Conway and Char Sligar (2002) capture the need for a communications program most effectively. They state:

> *Knowledge creators may view KM as a threat to their prestige, or perhaps even their livelihood. After all, if you are the only person who truly understands how to solve a particular issue, why should you be interested in sharing this knowledge? It dilutes your expertise, reduces your worth to the organization, and may mean that it can survive using less skilled (and hence less expensive) personnel. . . . To address this risk, an effective communications and recognition program MUST support any KM initiative. The truly innovative problem-solvers must appreciate that not only does their worth to the organization increase the more they share their knowledge and move on to solve new issues, but equally important, their managers understand their value (p. 70).*

This value proposition for sharing and reusing knowledge must be well communicated to all employees if the organization hopes to succeed with its goal of embedding new knowledge-based working habits.

Based on the need for a viable communications program to be in place, here are five areas you should focus on when setting corporate expectations around KM:

1. Corporate alignment: The aligning of KM work with the business drivers and strategic goals of the organization is fundamental to its likely success. Therefore, ensure

that all messaging that comes from the central KM group reinforces this symbiotic relationship as often as possible. In fact, it is acceptable to refer to all the business issues and desired outcomes more often than you do to the KM work that underpins it. Remember that perception is everything, and you want people to connect successful business outcomes with the application of KM tools and techniques. Let the business be seen to be driving KM, not the other way round.

2. Credible targets: Set an appropriate level of expectation around KM targets, so that senior managers will buy in to what you are trying to achieve. Above all, avoid anything enterprise-wide in scope if at all possible, especially the dreaded *changing the culture* black hole, as it will swallow you alive if you are not careful. Stick with a focus on business processes and try for a quick win, no matter how small. The old adage of underpromising and overdelivering is what you are aiming for. Keep it small, and leave the bigger business issues alone, at least until you have some business champions on board.

3. Clear language: Avoid jargon and find an appropriate level of language that is clear and consistent. If you cannot find a way to describe KM activity using normal business language, then do not. It is a sure kiss of death to your communications efforts if people start seeing the language you use to describe KM as being too esoteric and too difficult to easily understand.

4. Constant communications: Keep talking about KM. According to communications experts, the average individual needs to receive a message three times before he or she fully comprehends and digest it. This does not mean that you have to e-mail everyone in the organization with three e-mails a day describing the joys of KM. In fact the whole mass-communications issue is a thorny one.

How much is too much? Targeted communications are a much sounder bet. Look for communities of interest, subject experts, and managers who have expressed an interest in KM to form a group to which you send regular KM-based communications. Apart from that, use e-mail sparingly, people very often do not have the time or inclination to read these types of communication. Instead, look to inform employees on a regular basis through information sessions (e.g., lunch and learn, presentations to teams and communities, open-day sessions where practitioners can get together and present KM case studies, lessons learned, etc.).

5. Consultation and collaboration: Provide the tools and techniques for doing KM, and then let the various individuals and communities that use them become sharing, yet self-sustaining, entities. Look to develop a model of central alignment, e.g., common processes, methodologies etc., and de-centralized implementation, e.g., let business users deploy the tools and techniques in a way that best suits their individual requirements. To do this effectively you will need to form strong business partnerships and alignment with business units and users. You want to be viewed as collaborators, not dictators, in the eyes of your business community, and you want then to view you as the subject-experts who bring added value to them in solving their business problems.

Step six: Prepare for success

One of the easiest mistakes to make is scoping success beyond your reach, typically by proposing work on an enterprise-wide scale to your senior management for approval. So, as a follow on to setting a realistic level of expectation in the organization concerning the impact that KM will have on the business, it is equally important to set an expectation level around what success from implementing KM will look like. Remember that this is a high-level view of what constitutes success, and accordingly needs to point to outcomes that are fairly generic and strategic in nature. In other words, outcomes that are more qualitative than quantitative in nature. A more detailed view to measuring success through scorecards, or other similar measurement techniques, is covered in the next chapter.

So here are some high-level successful outcomes that you might want to consider, that essentially comprise the value proposition for KM in the organization:

1. Improvement of knowledge visibility—this outcome is based on the number of new ways in which the organization helps people to connect to corporate knowledge. It highlights the ways that are in use to improve knowledge access, such as knowledge repositories, search and navigation software, knowledge maps and directories, expertise locators, best practices and lessons learned catalogues, knowledge brokerage services, etc.

2. Improvement of knowledge intensity—this outcome is based on the number of new ways in which the organization helps to build knowledge depth. It highlights the ways that are in use to facilitate the creation and maintenance of knowledge communities and subject expertise, such as collaboration software, creation and maintenance processes for communities, learning and self-help opportunities, mentoring programs, etc.

3. Improvement of knowledge infrastructure—this outcome is based on the number of new ways in which the organization seeks to improve knowledge creation and sharing capacity. It especially highlights the use of technology

to improve the organization's ability to capture, store, retrieve, share, and maintain its knowledge assets.

4. Improvement of knowledge competence—this outcome is based on the number of new ways in which the organization helps people to manage knowledge more competently. It highlights the ways that are in use to improve knowledge-based work processes, such as fostering a learning and sharing culture through stated corporate goals and objectives, encouraging employees to share what they know with others and to leverage content from inside and outside the organization, an emphasis on growing knowledge-based competencies and skills, a rewards and recognition program for superior performance in managing knowledge assets.

The beauty of these four outcomes is that they are high-level enough to be equally effective whether the context is just a couple of examples of helping a work unit to inventory and manage its knowledge assets, or something grander spread across a business line or even the enterprise itself.

Take-away Menu

Here are 5 things worth remembering about deploying KM:

1. Make partnering your deployment mantra, and look to work with business units on practical opportunities to engage KM, no matter how small they might be.
2. Find points of stability in the organization and look for KM deployment opportunities there.
3. Work with cross-functional business teams to create a portfolio of knowledge-process templates that any business unit can use for capturing and sharing knowledge,

subject expertise, customer and project learning, best practices etc.

4. Let the pace and direction of KM deployment be dictated by business units rather than the KM community, and focus more on how KM can be relevant to the organization rather than where you think it should fit.

5. As you deploy KM, remember that nothing is new, and no one knows it all, so do not be afraid to change things around and take a different course based on new ideas and creative input from others in the organization.

SIX

Measuring Knowledge Management in the Organization

To IMPROVE IS TO CHANGE; TO BE PERFECT IS TO CHANGE OFTEN.

Winston Churchill

WHY MEASURE KNOWLEDGE MANAGEMENT?

Now that you are implementing knowledge management (KM) in your organization, you can start thinking about how you might want to measure its impact on the business. One of the first things you will want to clarify in your mind is whether you will attempt to formalize some sort of KM measurement program in the organization. The need to implement KM metrics has been a thorn in the side of many knowledge managers and has proved to be an insurmountable hurdle to many. It is not the fact that there are not plenty of prospective KM metrics around—in fact any quick search on the Internet will reveal many of them for your appraisal—it is just that not many people seem to be confident that any of them have any real business value. Remember that any measures you adopt generally have to be clearly understandable to all, resonate with your business managers, and avoid being seen as being too warm and fuzzy to have any real-world value. Quite a task when you think about it. However, despite the difficulty involved, you still need to develop some clear measures of success otherwise you will be unable to engage the KM stake holder community, or those business managers whose support KM, and resources you may be chasing. The bottom line is that no business manager is going to commit time and resources to something that they cannot see any quantifiable benefit in doing. The key is to find measures that resonate with the business and can be aligned with how other aspects of organizational business activity are measured. As Kaplan and Norton observe in *The Balanced Scorecard* (1996; p. 191), a measurement system enables a company to

> bridge a major gap that formerly existed: a fundamental disconnect between
> the development of strategy and its implementation.

So far there are not any generic metrics that have been developed and adopted as standard by the worldwide KM community. As C. Boyd said in an article on developing practical KM metrics in 2004, "Showing how the KM program benefits the firm is difficult because KM is a relatively new function and has virtually no standard success metrics" (p. 1). In the absence of any standardized approach to measurement, many organizations have invented a measurement system of their own. These range from the low level use of a few well-targeted volumetrics e.g., how many recognized knowledge communities there are in an organization, to the all-encompassing (e.g., complete enterprise-wide balanced scorecards for KM activity). However, many KM practitioners still seem to be struggling to make the connection between the work they do and the business objectives of the organization. Without this linkage it will be difficult to show where KM contributes value to the business community. It seems that most people fear corporate measurement because they see it as being synonymous with return on investment (ROI), and they are not sure how to link KM-based outcomes to ROI, especially from a public sector perspective where the goals of the organization are not profit-based at all. The public sector tends to equate ROI more on the level of services it provides to the citizen, and their corresponding level of satisfaction or dissatisfaction with those services. However, whereas the ultimate goal of measuring the effectiveness of a KM initiative may be to determine some type of ROI, there are many unknown variables that may affect the measurements you may choose. The first of these is that of deciding what your objectives are in wishing to measure KM, and in so doing decide how well those objectives align with the overarching objectives of the business. For instance, are you measuring solely to show the ROI on the initial investment, to help refine and improve KM processes, to help develop performance assessment benchmarks to use for future comparisons, to help develop a corporate business case for doing KM, or are you measuring all of them? Based on what you decide to measure, you will need to find a way to correlate KM activities with business outcomes, while not claiming too precise a cause-and-effect relationship.

Figure 6.1 shows an overview of the main organizational perspectives that KM is looking to provide improvement for. These four dimensions are fairly generic, but help provide a context for any potential measurement program. They are especially well aligned with the balanced scorecard approach to measurement.

Whatever your approach to developing KM metrics, it is a good idea to first adopt some overarching guiding principles to help ensure the measures you develop are both relevant to the business, and also effective. Here are some principles that can provide a framework for your measurement program to operate within:

- Anyone involved with delivering knowledge services should be able to articulate the business value of what they are delivering, and know how that value will be measured.

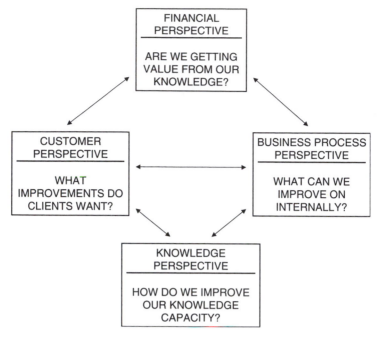

FIGURE 6.1   *Measurement perspectives for knowledge management.*

- Measurements should be consistent with organizational values and business objectives and align with any corporate strategies designed to facilitate better business-management practices.
- Any KM metrics should be seen as being part of an overall business measurement program and not be considered in isolation to other corporate metrics.
- Any KM metrics should be reviewed on a regular (yearly, or maybe every other year) basis by a focus group composed of business users and corporate KM to ensure their continuing relevance and alignment with the organization's goals and objectives.

At the same time as you are developing these overarching guidelines, you can look at a more focused set of questions that you should ask be asking before defining and developing each potential metric. Typically you need to know answers to the following questions:

- Who are the stakeholders involved and what is it that they want to know about?
- What is it that will be measured?
- What business objective does the metric align with and support?
- What, if any, technologies and techniques are required to provide a measurement?
- What mechanisms will be in place to analyze the measure and provide corrective actions if they are deemed necessary?
- What is needed to ensure adequate feedback and communications mechanisms are in place in response to measurement data?

Once you have established answers to these questions you are better able to understand the design and measurement components that you will need. It also goes without saying that even if you have a willing stake holder and a clear understanding of what will be measured, you will probably still need a positive answer to the third question concerning alignment with business objectives. Its not that you cannot proceed without this alignment being in place, but if you are wise you will want to take a long look at what the real benefits to the business will be if you should proceed without it. There may be extenuating circumstances where you feel it is in everyone's interest to proceed, but generally if you cannot find a compelling business rationale for measuring something, then do not.

Finally, before deciding on which metrics you will use, you should always consider that they will need to show whether knowledge is being captured, shared, and reused and whether the use of the information provided has improved service quality

or operational efficiency. You will probably also want to develop
some measures that can underpin component pieces of your KM
strategy, if at all possible. For example, if part of your KM strategy is to facilitate better corporate knowledge sharing, you should
find a way to measure the activity around knowledge-community
evolution in the organization.

Whichever metrics you select, you will also need to provide an
organizational context, a storyline if you like, for the measurement program, one that will allow for a common level of understanding as to the why, the what, and the how of the measurements
themselves. For example, the American Department of the Navy
contexts their KM metrics within three different types of measurement domains: outcomes, outputs, and systems. This seems
to me to be a fairly business-oriented approach and one that
should appeal to most business managers. However, some prefer
a somewhat softer edge to measurement and context their programs through a less business-focused lens, with more emphasis
on corporate culture. Either approach can be suitable, it depends
on where your organization's focus is and what business issues it
believes it needs to address through the application of KM.

WHAT MIGHT YOU MEASURE?

Metrics typically fall into one of two categories: The data are
qualitative or quantitative in nature. Quantitative measures tend
to focus on areas where you want to evaluate performance or spot
developing trends or patterns—the number of people accessing
a particular source of information, for example. Qualitative
measures can also be used to highlight trends and patterns, and
they can also help provide context and meaning for quantitative
measures—for example, how knowledge derived from accessing
a source of information helped address a business issue. A good
approach is to attempt a balance of quantitative and qualitative,

a mix of the anecdotal and evidential if you like. Both can be powerful tools in illustrating the benefits of doing KM, depending on which type of audience you are addressing and what their interest in KM is likely to be. Having a balance of the two types of metrics will help strengthen KM's profile and appeal on the business and personal levels.

Remember that no metric can be applied directly to happiness, but in essence that is what you are trying to measure, the happiness (or satisfaction) of the individual or the organization in relation to the use of KM. So to help you get under way, here

TABLE 6.1   *Checklist for Optimizing Organizational KM Activity*

Business Domain	Measurements
Strategy and leadership	• Effective KM strategies are defined. • KM initiatives are linked to strategies. • Senior managers are accountable for KM. • Clear organizational objectives are established for KM. • Senior managers actively promote the creation, capture, sharing, and reuse of information.
Performance and motivation	• Performance is measured against customer expectations and satisfaction levels. • Mechanisms are in place to capture lessons learned and best practices from KM work, and reapply them in future program or project work. • Usage statistics for portals, Intranets, knowledge systems and repositories are captured. • The central KM group is consulted by business units for analysis, planning, and process knowledge-enablement purposes. • Performance reviews include knowledge-based competencies such as sharing, reuse, and mentoring.

(Continued)

TABLE 6.1 *Continued*

Business Domain	Measurements
Current competencies and future capabilities	• Knowledge sharing and reuse activity are recognized and rewarded. • KM training for employees is encouraged, and the number of participants is tracked. • KM competency is a component of corporate retention and hiring strategies. • Knowledge mapping and ease of access to knowledge expertise are facilitated. • Client satisfaction levels and feedback are used as a basis for evaluating future competency and skills requirements.
Culture and climate	• Mentoring programs are in place. • Adequate resources are allocated to help achieve KM goals and objectives. • A culture that encourages collaboration and sharing of ideas and knowledge is in place. • Success stories, lessons learned, and best practices are showcased and promoted in the organization. • Alliances with other organizations are formed for mutual benefit and the growth of knowledge capacity.
Communication and communities	• Participation in communities of practice or interest is facilitated, and increases in community numbers are measured. • A communications plan for explaining and promoting KM activity exists. • Knowledge awareness sessions (e.g., open days, case studies, seminars, best practice presentations) are held. • Online communities are equipped with effective information technology tools to facilitate the capture, communication, and sharing of ideas, information, and knowledge. • Open and timely communications are encouraged as a normal business practice.

KM, knowledge management.

(in no particular semblance of order or priority) the following sections represent some areas for metrics you might want to consider to help you kick-start your measurement work.

These five metrics domains cover a good mix of business and people-focused outcomes, all of which can be used as the basis for some more detailed measures. They are by no means a comprehensive list, but they should get you thinking about what is relevant to your business, and what would be a good fit for your organization. It does not matter if none of these areas resonate particularly well with your business community, as most organizations will customize their requirements anyway, and there are no rights or wrongs here. The only issue you need to consider is what will stand the scrutiny of your senior managers and what can best represent your KM efforts in a positive light from a business perspective. Also it is worth remembering that generally, numbers tend to hold a greater power of persuasion in people's minds than do anecdotal measures, so aim to couch any measures in numeric terms or percentages, wherever possible.

How Will You Measure?

Once you have made a decision as to what your metrics are going to be, you will need to make a decision on what mechanism you will choose to actually measure them. There are a number of possibilities you could consider: a corporate KM capacity check or audit, a balanced scorecard approach, a customized matrix of home-grown measures, or a strategic measurement framework aligned with business goals. I am sure that there are plenty of other ways of measuring, but these four should provide you with some practical choices to be going on with.

1. A KM capacity check, or audit
   Many organizations start with this activity when undertaking KM measurement programs. Why? Because

if you want to know where you are going from a KM perspective, you need to know where you are now in terms of knowledge capabilities and performance. Performing a knowledge capacity check or audit can help an organization determine what knowledge needs it has and what knowledge capacity it has to address those needs. The gap analysis that such data can produce is extremely useful in helping to craft the organization's knowledge strategy, goals, and objectives and can form the basis of any KM plan going-forward.

While I was at Public Works and Government Services Canada (PWGSC) we (the KM group) performed a departmental KM maturity survey. To my knowledge, this remains the only time such a survey has been performed in a major Canadian government department and to say it produced mixed results would be an understatement. We encountered a full spectrum of responses, ranging from those where respondents professed a complete ignorance of the subject matter (KM), to those where respondents filled page after page with responses that were only barely connected to the subject matter, to those were respondents endorsed KM in the strongest way imaginable. We even had one business unit refuse to participate, and I was roundly abused (at least that's my recollection) for having the temerity to suggest they waste their valuable time on anything so frivolous! It was also a fact that we spent more time explaining the questions and the whole philosophy behind the survey than we did analyzing the responses. The message was clear: We had not prepared well enough in the first place.

Therefore, if you want to succeed with any capacity check or survey, you had better start by thinking how you can prepare the organization for it as well as you possibly can. The reason for this is that there is still a fairly low level of understanding around KM, and few, if any, business managers see the value in finding out the organization's capacity for it. What this invariably means is that they will not participate or will delegate the responsibility to someone else who may have only a limited background in the discipline. And what that means is that your data may not be substantive enough, or even relevant enough, to warrant drawing any conclusions from it at a strategic level. So, be prepared to spend time in coaching business units on the reasons why a check is a good idea and in providing them with a common understanding of KM terminology and some helpful suggestions on how they might want to respond to questions.

If you do decide to proceed with a capacity check approach, there are a number of business areas you can consider for inclusion. The Canadian Institute of Knowledge Management (CIKM) developed the KM Maturity Survey that we did at PWGSC with questions in the following areas:

- Knowledge planning
- Knowledge retention
- Knowledge sharing and reuse
- Knowledge processes
- Knowledge tools
- Knowledge culture

Knowledge planning was focused on embedding KM into organizational planning, and looked at progress in implementing governance models, centers of expertise, and communities of practice and in organizing knowledge both vertically and horizontally.

Knowledge retention was focused on embedding KM into human resources (HR) and looked at progress in implementing KM into HR planning, management, and succession planning and in workforce sustainment and hiring criteria.

Knowledge sharing and reuse were focused on the leveraging of intellectual assets and looked at progress in advocating the use and reuse of corporate knowledge assets, in implementing measurements for the use and reuse of knowledge, and in the management of intellectual capital, best practices, and lessons learned.

Knowledge processes was focused on embedding KM into process engineering and looked at progress in implementing KM analysis methods, fast look-up, and advanced research capabilities and in embedding integrated feedback systems and KM into people-focused and technology-focused processes.

Knowledge tools were focused on KM planning, implementing, and collaborating technologies and looked at progress in implementing decision matrices, social network analysis tools, business intelligence tools, metadata management tools, and workplace collaboration tools.

Knowledge culture was focused on building bridges between islands of corporate knowledge and looked at progress in implementing knowledge policies, rewards, and recognition programs and in defining business drivers for KM and in identifying internal knowledge domains and internal KM champions and stakeholders.

Whatever you eventually decide to focus on for your capacity check, make sure you have a game plan in mind for how you will communicate the results and in how you will use the data to align your KM activities with organizational hot spots and areas of need. Remember that a positive spin (i.e., "Here are the many opportunities the capacity check has identified for progress on business front") as opposed to a negative spin (i.e., "Here are all the things you are not doing well that you need KM for") will go a long way to helping make your check seem more relevant in the eyes of the business community.

2. A Balanced scorecard
Balanced scorecards are intended to provide a multi-layered view of organizational performance, one that looks at internal business processes, customer satisfaction from an operational perspective, financial stability, the history of business changes already made, and the potential improvement measures which can help drive future performance. Or, as Kaplan and Norton describe it in *The Balanced Scorecard* (1996; p. 29),

> *The balanced scorecard translates vision and strategy into objectives and measures across a balanced set of perspectives . . . [It] measures . . . performance across four perspectives: financial, customers, internal business processes and learning and growth.*

In essence, the balanced scorecard seeks to align measures with corporate strategies to enable progress to be tracked and to help ensure accountability and prioritize areas of potential improvement. Many business managers are attracted by the intent of the balanced scorecard, which is to help select measures that can maintain a balance between short-term and long-term business objectives, financial and nonfinancial investments, and external and internal performance dynamics. The pay back from a well-crafted balanced scorecard is that it can be used as much as a communications medium as a measurement tool and through its application can help create a shared understanding of the corporate vision while communicating the business' objectives and strategies to the organization as a whole. In so doing, it can be very useful in helping employees see how and where they contribute to organizational success by linking personal outcomes with the scorecard's organizational measurements.

So what might elements might a balanced scorecard for KM contain? Here are some ideas for you to consider, based on an approach that looks at the following four business domains; finance, clients, processes and employees:

Finance: Possible metrics could include revenue growth, cost reduction, accounting timeframes, asset utilization, quality and timeliness of financial processes (e.g., customer billing, accounts payable, budget management, payroll, ledgers, journals, etc.).

Clients: Possible metrics could include customer acquisition, customer retention, customer satisfaction, customer service quality and timeliness, profitability rates, responsiveness rates, repeat business ratio, and so forth.

Processes: Possible metrics could include product or service-development processes (e.g., time to review, time to develop, time to verify, time to market, time to respond, etc.), operational processes (e.g., order processing, supply and shipment, problem resolution, inventory control, quality and maintenance, etc.).

Employees: Possible metrics could include idea generation, competencies growth, employee retention, employee satisfaction, absenteeism rates, workforce diversity, and communities growth, development programs (e.g., mentoring, succession planning, etc.).

There are many other potential metrics you could use, but the important thing is to find the right balance between the domains you choose. Most organizations that have implemented a balanced scorecard program seem to think it a good investment in time and resources—an investment that can help align KM with the organization's strategic objectives and show how KM can help in achieving those objectives. However, be warned that setting up a balanced scorecard program takes a lot of investment in time and effort, not just from the KM group, but from the whole organization. The setting up of the collection and collation of measurement data to feed the scorecard requires a high degree of commitment from the business units involved. Accordingly, while a balanced scorecard may prove an effective guidance tool, it is unlikely that many organizations will set one up just to measure KM progress and future potential. However, it is quite likely that where a balanced scorecard already exists, or one is to be built, that KM can fit in there as a subcomponent.

3.   A customized matrix

A customized matrix is the measurements tool most often used by organizations planning to implement KM programs. Although other approaches may seem to be too complex and labor-intensive, a set of customized measures makes a lot of sense from a resource point of view. In some ways, it is a parallel activity to the capacity check, although one that seeks to measure on a continual basis not just as a one-off. You could describe this kind of approach as being a corporate dashboard or operational early-warning radar. What you are essentially building is a set of customized measurements that simply and clearly illustrate where and how KM is having an impact in the organization. The operative word here is simple and the more straightforward the measures are, the better. You want to make them easy to understand, regardless of what audience is seeing them, and easy to measure and do comparisons against.

To begin with you should consider how such a matrix fits from a strategic point of view and finding that fit will help you target something that will be well understood and meaningful to your business community. Consider these three areas for measurement: how is knowledge being used in the organization currently, whether the use of that knowledge is producing optimal value for the organization, and, how well is the organization prepared for using knowledge in the future.

Current knowledge use: Possible metrics could include: usage statistics for knowledge portals, Intranets and repositories, number of best practices captured, number of best practices applied in the organization, number of employees taking KM-based training courses, number of employees involved in communities of practice or interest, number of business processes where KM has been applied, number of programs or projects using KM tools and techniques, etc.

Knowledge and value: Possible metrics could include number of knowledge maps or directories available for access to knowledge and subject expertise, number of KM-based technology tools available, number of programs or projects requesting KM expertise form the central KM group, employee satisfaction ratings concerning knowledge activities such as search and retrieval, availability of knowledge sources, and so forth.

Future knowledge use: Possible metrics could include internal capabilities assessments (gap identification), mentoring programs usage, usage of knowledge directories or maps, client and employee satisfaction feedback mechanisms, and so forth.

A customized matrix will give the organization plenty of latitude to measure at whatever scale and pace they decide is appropriate. Above all, any such matrix is completely scaleable and easy to manage. These virtues should not be ignored as measurements have an unhappy knack of taking over your life, sucking away time and energy that could be devoted to other KM activity.

4. A strategic framework for measurement

A strategic framework is intended to provide KM metrics that can be seen as being supporting measures to specifically targeted strategic imperatives. For example, the senior manager or managers might periodically review the key environmental factors that are affecting the organization and decide on what the strategically important outcomes would be for the company in response to these factors. For example, a loss in market or customer base might lead to a commitment from the organization's leaders to achieve a growth in earnings of 10% for the subsequent year. Once the various commitments are decided upon, the organization's business units are then expected to identify what initiatives they will undertake in support of these commitments. At the same time, the business units are expected to identify what measurement criteria they will apply against each initiative to help gauge its level of success and its contribution to the overall strategy. KM is just one of the areas that will provide its measurements in support of the targeted outcomes. All of the measurements are then integrated into a comprehensive variable pay program, where increases in pay are linked to achieving successful outcomes.

The benefit of this approach is that measures are focused on a small, core set of projects that impact everyone in the organization. What that tends to mean is that people become extremely focused on achieving successful outcomes for all of the component measurement areas, including KM. The bottom line here is that everyone succeeds or fails together, and there is nothing like the thought of failure hurting people financially to focus minds and energies. There is nothing wrong with such an approach, although it has to be realized that KM will not be the focus of the program, just one more area that contributes to it. In other words, you may get some quick attention for KM but you are not likely to get any long-term strategic commitments to KM or be able to focus on any KM activity that is not in the small set of strategic initiatives. This might be a smart thing to do if you want to gain some corporate profile, and to get a limited set of KM activities underway in the organization. But do not look to this approach if you want to focus on anything broader or deeper than that.

Now you have decided on which measurements tool you will use, you need to consider how you will collect and collate any data that you capture, and above all, how you will package and promote the results within the organization. If you have aligned the work well with your business' objectives, you will find that business units are more than willing to publicize any good-news stories that result from your measurement activities. After all, if business units already feel that their success measures align with your KM-based ones, it will be their own success that they will be publicizing anyway, and from that standpoint they will feel much happier in crediting KM with a supporting role in any successful outcomes that have been achieved.

Finally, there is a significant opportunity waiting amid all this measurement activity. If you can help provide measurable feedback on the success of individual initiatives by correlating KM metrics with specific internal marketing or change management activities, then you can broaden both the scope and impact of any KM measurement program you might undertake.

TAKE-AWAY MENU

Here are five things worth remembering about measuring KM:

1. Whatever the scale of your measurement and assessment efforts, whether large or small, make sure that your measures are grounded in sound business logic, contain business language, and are easily understandable, both in their use of language and in the purpose they convey.

2. If a measure cannot be linked to a business objective somehow, do not consider using it.

3. If you have a choice, I would recommend you use more quantitative than qualitative measures. Because no matter how truthful or not they really are, numbers will tell your story far more convincingly to senior managers than soft measures can. However you should use a mixture of quantitative and qualitative metrics to show value across the whole organization.

4. Look to broaden the scope of your measurement program by correlating KM metrics with specific internal marketing or change management activities, to provide measurable feedback on the success of specific individual initiatives.

5. If you want to keep your measurements relevant and focused, make sure you schedule regular review processes that involve your stakeholder community.

PART III

MAKING THE CONNECTION: LESSONS FROM THE FRONT LINE

SEVEN

Lessons Learned

Some the Hard Way

EXPERIENCE IS THE NAME EVERYONE GIVES TO THEIR MISTAKES.

Oscar Wilde

To avoid the mistakes of the past, we are told we should learn the lessons of history. Sounds reasonable, but wasn't it Henry Ford who said "history is more or less bunk"? At the risk of alienating those who believe firmly in the first maxim, I tend to side with Mr. Ford's view of things when it comes to expecting lessons learned to be the key to the potential success of any knowledge management (KM) initiative. Yet, learning from the lessons of others would seem to be the easiest way for any KM practitioner to gain expertise and street smarts. After all, if you can absorb the lessons that others have learned, benefit from their successes, and avoid their costly mistakes, you should be onto a winner, right? Not necessarily.

Lessons learned are somewhat like those miracle diets we see advertised on television—replete with the promise of providing us with the solution to a problem we are unable to tackle alone. Just like those too-good-to-be-true dietary cures, the truth is that absorbing lessons learned will only ever provide us with a partial solution to our KM problems. There still remains the little issue of actually having to do something for ourselves to have any hope of achieving our miracle cure. The problem with KM lessons is that each is stamped with its own unique flavor in terms of time, place, intention, and organizational and personnel parameters. Any one of the aforementioned may prove to have been a unique circumstance that will prevent the outcome from ever being reproduced entirely. This is why context is so critical to knowledge retention. Knowledge without the context of how, why, when, and where it was created is knowledge of a lesser value.

This does not mean that lessons learned, with or without the proper context, have no value to us. In fact, lessons are always worth consideration before proceeding with any KM planning or deployment activities. Comparisons to lessons learned that are out of context may be unhelpful, but in the case of operationalizing KM for your own organization, comparisons in context can be extremely helpful. Therefore, it is crucial to ensure you do your comparisons well before proceeding. Be realistic and decide what is or is not applicable on the basis of what your operational parameters actually are, not on what you would like them to be based on someone else's success story. It may seem self-evident to say you should start by trying to compare yourself against others who have implemented KM in a similar-sized organization, with similar business processes, and a similar culture; however, I am always amazed by the number of people who attempt to use the KM experiences of others from completely disparate types of organizations as a roadmap for their own endeavors. The rationale seems to be that if it worked well for Siemens, for example, with hundreds of thousands of employees, it should work well for their own organizations even though they are fundamentally different from Siemens in every conceivable way. This type of comparison makes no sense to me; it seems to be setting yourself up for failure before you even get started.

What you will read in this chapter are some lessons learned—a few of them the hard way—after a number of years of deploying KM in major government organizations. The more I have seen of KM endeavors, the more I have become convinced that there is one strong common denominator to all these lessons learned: human behavior. The lessons in this chapter are really more a chronicle of what does or does not work at the human level, rather than a chronicle of what does or does not work at an organizational level. The distinction may seem subtle, but is in fact profound. While new business fads and organizational imperatives may come and go, basic human nature remains as a common thread throughout differing organizations. Knowledge of the human factor can become your most effective predictor of possible success or failure, much more so than the more obvious and usual business indicators that accompany any new initiative, such as the availability of adequate resources or the commitment of senior management.

The lessons learned in this chapter highlight some of the Canadian government's work that I have been involved in and experiences gained from private-sector organizations that I worked for or am connected to on a personal basis. It sometimes seems that too many people start out with the sole intention of winning an enterprise-wide campaign for KM. My belief is that it is far more important to win some of the daily battles at work and let the campaign take care of itself. These lessons are reflections on some of those battles.

LESSON 1: KNOWLEDGE MANAGEMENT STRATEGY IS REALLY BUSINESS STRATEGY

In 2003, a survey by KPMG of several hundred European businesses found that more than 80 percent of senior mangers surveyed considered knowledge to be a strategic asset in their organizations. Yet, an equal number were unable to define what a KM strategy should look like. So it seems there is plenty of room for the development of KM strategies. However, it is important to realize that there are two dimensions to be addressed here: One is the development of the KM strategy itself, the other is the alignment of any KM strategy to that of the organization. In other words, the KM strategy is inextricably linked to the business strategy. Sounds obvious, does it not? Well despite it seeming to be so obvious, many KM strategies are far too one-dimensional and focused more on the desired outcomes of the KM practitioners in the organization than on the desired business outcomes of the organization. Unfortunately, studies show that alignment with business strategy is neither a motivating factor nor a key evaluation criterion of KM initiatives in most companies. This invariably means that KM work becomes disconnected from the real business issues that need to be resolved.

The goal of KM should not be self-serving. It is far more important to deal with an organization's pressing business issues and find out how KM can facilitate addressing them than it is to ensure KM is deployed in the organization. If you do the former well, it is likely that the latter will happen as a matter of course. So, how do you establish knowledge as a supporting capability to the business strategy? The first step is to think of knowledge alignment from two perspectives: the perspective of the development of a business strategy and the perspective of supporting the strategy once it is developed.

Developing the business strategy: Based on an approach where strategy equals organizational capabilities, knowledge plays a pivotal role in building the capabilities and the organizational capacity necessary to develop further capabilities and competencies. Strategic capabilities that knowledge helps to create and maintain are typically value innovation, environmental understanding, experimentation, design capacity, predictive activity, and organizational memory. Through these types of activities it becomes easier for an organization to identify clearly the way that knowledge enables strategy development and future maintenance.

Supporting the business strategy: This is a more straightforward value proposition, as knowledge plays a unique and visible role in support of desired business outcomes, especially from the standpoint of enhancing the operational infrastructure from which an organization's services and products are delivered. Particularly significant in this tactical context is knowledge used to support business performance and knowledge used to support business productivity. Knowledge-based activities in support of business performance are typically managing customer knowledge, building organizational knowledge processes, identifying knowledge and information linkages, and aggregation of organizational learning. Knowledge-based activities in support of business productivity are typically capturing and sharing best practices and other reusable knowledge assets, promotion of knowledge-based practices and processes, and coordination and management of organizational knowledge and information repositories.

The most successful KM strategies are well aligned with an overarching business strategy and tend to focus on smaller, manageable projects that help deliver one supporting capability at a time, rather than trying to address all strategic elements at once.

The crucial lesson to be learned here is that there is no such thing as a supportable stand-alone KM strategy and if you are the owner of such a thing you had better rethink your approach—and quickly.

LESSON 2: DEFINITIONAL WARS—DO NOT DIE ON THAT HILL

Defining KM should be fairly straightforward. At least you would think so, wouldn't you? In fact this definition can prove to be the single biggest impediment to early progress as you get a KM initiative under way. It is surprising how emotional people become when it comes to defining KM and how confrontational these definition warriors can become. The quicksand of definition will swallow you alive if you are not careful.

The truth is that everyone perceives KM differently and each is likely to have a different definition for KM, or at least a different understanding of what it means. An invitation to define KM can quickly turn into your worst nightmare. I have seen meetings degenerate on the basis of differing definitions. I try to avoid defining KM at meetings. Instead I ask the same question back to anyone who asks me how I define KM and then agree with them as it is often the easiest and quickest way to avoid potential conflict and move on to more important and interesting topics.

However, the central KM function in the organization will still need to supply a common understanding of KM. Focus on providing a vision and objectives for KM from an organizational perspective to ensure a common understanding of what KM is all about and let individual business units describe what that will mean (i.e., a definition for their doing KM, from their own perspectives). To avoid becoming ensnared in a definitional war, find out your organization's real requirement for doing KM and always define it in those terms. This will enable you to describe what you think KM will do for the organization, not what you think it is—a subtle difference, but one that should help you avoid the definitional issue to some extent, as most definition warriors are focused on trying to describe KM. For example, here is how we described KM at Public Works and Government Services Canada (PWGSC), "A discipline and organizational strategy for ensuring that corporate knowledge is identified, captured, created, shared and used to improve and maintain the services that we deliver to our clients." This definition covers all the bases that deal with the life cycle of knowledge and specifically the commitment to improve delivery of services to clients, which was the organization's strategic goal at the time. This definition may seem bland and too generic to some, but it is also nonthreatening, does not challenge people too deeply, and states something that few would disagree with. Most important, few people would want to be seen to disagree with it. A rule of thumb that can usually be applied to definitions is that if you can tell it to anyone in the organization, even someone who has never heard of KM, and they understand it and how it applies to your business, it stands a fair chance of being successful.

The reality is that definitions do not really matter in the long run. It is far better to leave enough room for interpretation, and even customization in a definition, if that keeps everyone happy. A generic and high-level definition is also far preferable from a business-unit perspective as it can usually fit nicely into the business-unit's own view of where knowledge is important from the perspective of its business goals and strategies.

The crucial lesson to be learned here is that too precise a definition of KM will likely constrain your organization, especially the individuals in it, from being able to be flexible and adaptable in response to the need to manage knowledge.

LESSON 3: NOT EVERYONE THINKS SURVEYS ARE SEXY

KM surveys often seem a logical way to proceed. After all, we need to know what an organization's capacity is for doing KM. However, if not properly positioned, KM surveys are likely to do more harm than good. A basic tenet of human nature is that we do not like to be told we are not doing something well or indeed that we are not doing it at all. There are also serious concerns about survey fatigue. Too many surveys that demand too much time and attention quickly cause employees to become indifferent. Just because you think surveys are a good idea, does not mean that everyone else will recognize their value. Undertake plenty of marketing and explaining before you start any survey and ensure the survey is easy to understand, simple to respond to, and delivers a clear sense of what it is trying to achieve.

Having said that, I have absolutely no doubt about the power of well-focused metrics; they have a clear and concise dimension to them that appeals to most senior managers. Explain at length about how poorly integrated feedback systems are being embedded and you will likely get a roomful of yawns. Tell senior managers that the maturity of knowledge processes in their organization rates a one on a scale of one to five and they understand instantly.

If you want to ensure success, you will need to have a clear idea of what you want to do with the data you collect from any survey. In my case, lack of a clear game plan was the single biggest failure of a survey we conducted on knowledge maturity at PWGSC. The data we collected were unique across the whole government of Canada, and yet we did not maximize them in a way that substantially moved the KM yardsticks forward.

Remember, surveys are not sexy unless you take their outcomes and turn them into a storyline that appeals to people. In fact, these outcomes may need to become several storylines, as what will be of interest to senior managers is not necessarily the same as what will be of interest to your knowledge community.

The crucial lesson to be learned here is to prepare your post-survey communications plan as carefully as you prepare your survey plan itself.

LESSON 4: MEASUREMENT IS A RELATIVE TERM

If you want to implement KM successfully in your organization you really have no option but to find a way to measure the benefits. Because every senior manager will want to know, "What is the return on our investment, and what did we gain?" It was the problem of trying to find an adequate answer to that question that first got me looking at ways to work under the corporate radar when promoting KM. Thus, *stealth KM* became the adopted approach for my team. However, the crucial question you will need to ask before proceeding with any KM metrics program is "how much, and how visibly, do I want to measure?"

It is not that you cannot measure KM, it is just that all the methods I have heard of, or tried myself, have not left me feeling confident that they will stand up to scrutiny, especially when pitched to someone like a chief financial officer (CFO). Unfortunately KM measurement tends to be of the soft and fuzzy kind: enhanced service delivery, improved innovation, better decision-making capacity, and so forth. These types of measurements do not identify readily with dollars from a senior manger's perspective. The lesson here is do not even bother trying to sell KM metrics at the senior management table. It is preferable never to have to ask senior managers for anything, either dollars or resources, where KM is concerned. The place to sell KM in your organization and the place to measure it is at the business-unit level. This is where you will find the real owners of your business—those who are tasked with delivering products and services. Here is where KM can find a natural home—in the operational requirement to improve processes and retain customers. By working on KM at the business-unit level you are going to achieve two things: First, you will shift the focus of measurement away from your internal KM organization; second, you will be able to attach KM success metrics directly to hard-nosed business metrics such as increased product volume, improved work processes and enhanced client satisfaction. The implication is clear: The successes of business units will by association also become the successes of KM and will help to establish the business value proposition for KM.

Furthermore, working on measurements at a business-unit level allows a degree of customization to meet unique requirements and a fuller sense of ownership by business managers of the measures and their accompanying results. Some of the most successful measurements I have used include portal—Intranet or repository—usage statistics; numbers of people participating in communities of practice or interest; improved customer response times or MTTR (mean time to repair) statistics; satisfaction surveys (used in a targeted and discretionary way) for customers and employees; numbers of best practices contributed; numbers of KM success stories; and numbers of people taking KM training courses. This is by no means an all-inclusive list, but should give some idea of what might work in your organization.

If no KM-type measurements seem to work, try and ensure that KM is seen as an enabling function to business processes that are already being measured. The benefit to such an approach is that any failures in business delivery are not likely to be seen as failures of KM, but rather as failings from a business-process perspective. This symbiotic relationship between KM and business-unit processes is an ideal way to let KM be valued and measured by any organization.

As with Lesson 2, a crucial final step in your measurements program must be a communications plan for the metrics you have collected. The evidence shows that making metrics visible is an essential component of any effective measurement program. You will need to gauge carefully how receptive your organization is to bad news before you decide to broadcast any negative metrics. However, if managed appropriately, negative results can become a strong catalyst for change. If necessary, sugarcoat the *pill* and focus on the positive outcomes of your measurements program, ones that can most easily be reinforced going forward.

The crucial lesson to be learned here is to use metrics with discretion; they are only as good and as effective as the storyline around them enables them to be. Metrics should be used most frequently when it is necessary to gather or maintain momentum for KM work, especially at a process level. Metrics can be your ally when applied wisely, but do not expect them to effect large-scale changes in organizational direction and culture.

LESSON 5: PERCEPTION IS KING

This lesson is about communications, and more especially about how best to communicate the organizational benefits of doing KM. Begin by thinking small. This does not mean think in a small way; rather it means keep a sense of proportion in any initial KM planning. Remember, the initial focus is on something practical, something that can be successful, and most of all, something that you can use for good publicity. Whether you see it as publicity or propaganda, the intent is the same, to ensure a positive impression is created about KM. In fact, publicity and propaganda can be seen in a similar light when you think about it. Webster's defines propaganda as "ideas, facts, or allegations spread deliberately to further one's cause," which is pretty much what you are after. A successful outcome of any KM initiative is to present KM to your organization in a positive and empowering sense, and if that means spreading a little good news a long way, go for it.

However, before you can think about selling KM to too broad an audience, you need to have implemented at least one KM initiative successfully. The size of the initiative is immaterial; eventually no one will remember how big or small it was, only that it was a success. In a hard-nosed business world, only success will help create a positive perception of KM. If you have a KM failure, do not dwell on it and do not broadcast it to all. Find out quickly why the initiative failed—and be honest about your role in its failure—and quickly apply any lessons learned.

This is not deception; rather, it is pragmatism and good business management.

Finally, do not think you have to take on everything alone. The more you spread the load, the better your chances of creating a successful impression. Look for KM champions within your organization to be publicists of any successes. After all, no one has more credibility than those who have seen beneficial results first hand. The best testimonials are from real business users of KM tools and techniques.

The crucial lesson to be learned here is that it may be easy for skeptics to dismiss the KM work you are doing as being of low value and too impractical to implement. It is next to impossible for them to dismiss KM when it is showing positive results and winning testimonials from those who manage the business.

Lesson 6: Information Management versus Knowledge Management: It Is Not Always What It Seems

One of the things I have observed first hand is the way differing communities in an organization create barriers, either artificial or real, around themselves and the work they do. They do so often to ensure they keep the work they do to themselves, and by so doing make it difficult for outsiders to understand what they do and therefore to interfere with it. This can be a double-edged sword and is a risky ploy in today's flattened organizations, where senior managers expect to see more ubiquity of processes and business rules. A good example of this is the near demise of the records management community in the Canadian government over the last 10 years. Without a high profile, and without much understanding of what they did for the organization, records management functions became a favorite target for cuts and downsizing in many departments and agencies during the 1990s. Only the increased attention that the new millennium brought to information management (IM) made it apparent that departments and agencies were in trouble. They had severely diminished their ability to manage the information over which they had stewardship on behalf of the citizens of Canada. The result has been that over the last 5 years the Canadian government has had to spend time and resources in an attempt to rectify the problem it created in the first place. At the same time, the IM community has seen its profile and credentials suddenly raised, and for the first time has begun to see the work it does being regarded as important to the well-being of the public sector.

The KM community has also begun to establish a profile, albeit at a very low level. The KM community in relation to the IM community now finds itself in very much the role that the IM community had not long ago in relation to the information technology (IT) community: that of junior partner. This has led to some inevitable entrenchment, and also to more than a little reluctance by senior managers to embrace anything new (KM) that might distract from a barely established IM direction. The truth is that if you do IT and IM in an organization, you have laid the groundwork for KM, whether you recognize it or not. In fact, investing in IT and IM without leveraging the potential benefits of KM is definitely not smart business practice. IT lays a technology foundation on which IM practices and systems can be built, but the true payback will be when we use these systems and processes to enable knowledge to be captured, shared and re-used in our organizations.

What all this means is that most organizations are enabling the conditions for doing KM, even if they do not consider that they are actually doing KM. Therefore, if KM has to take a subservient profile to IM to achieve some traction, do not worry about it. Instead of spending time and energy trying to show how KM is different from IM, a far better strategy is to let KM play a supporting role to IM and IT. A desire to define the difference between IM and KM seems to be almost an obsession with some people in IM and KM communities. Personally I have never worried much about those kinds of lines of demarcation and have often deliberately blurred them to achieve a more inclusive view of the work that the different communities contribute organizationally. The issue of IM versus KM has two clear dimensions: first, the definition itself, which will suck time and energy out of you; and second, the potential for a great leap forward for KM, which can be achieved by playing this one smart. Let me explain.

I am a great believer in finding the path of least resistance, and if achieving KM goals means having to put KM work in an IM wrapper, then so be it. At PWGSC, I invariably used IM deployment as the main theme in any of my KM presentations. This had a number of advantages: It allowed the IM community to feel good about itself as a leader in the organization and it enabled KM to find a place at the table without too much fear of being seen as threatening or another unwanted overhead. This strategy plays well with managers who have already made a commitment to invest in IM, as they inevitably see it as a potential double payback.

The crucial lesson to be learned here is that you still have to ensure that KM-type work actually gets done and that people do not falsely believe that if they do IM, they must also be doing KM. In that sense, there is a difference that needs to be emphasized. However, the storyline is straightforward: IM infrastructure (systems and processes) is the foundation upon which a framework for knowledge mobilization can and should be built.

LESSON 7: "KNOWLEDGE MANAGEMENT IS NOT ABOUT TECHNOLOGY": WELL, ACTUALLY IT IS

The above statement was made to me once by a member of the government KM community when we were discussing barriers to KM implementation. On reflection, it seems to me that much of what constitutes the true barrier to successful KM implementation is contained in that one sentence. Consider the following: People like technology and they are usually happy to try something that makes their work easier. People's love of new technology is a factor that should not be ignored. How did half the planet end up swamped by e-mail and unable to keep up with the never-ending deluge of communication that comes our way? It was not because people wanted that condition to be the result of implementing e-mail technology, it was more that they wanted to fulfill a basic human need—communicating with others—and technology gave them the tools to fulfill that need. Whatever the reason, we all got sucked into the e-mail black hole. The message is plain, people just love to use technology, whatever its drawbacks.

So pervasive has this use of smart tools become that another KM-type function, instant messaging, looks like becoming the next technology tsunami. Instant messaging and indeed e-mail itself are as pure a stream of KM activity as you can find: capturing, sharing, and reusing each others' knowledge as we communicate with the world. The next time someone tells you that KM is not about technology, remind them that from a purely operational sense, technology is just about all that it is in many organizations.

KM practitioners have spent too much time trying to position KM as a new way of managing knowledge assets, when in fact technology has already beaten them to it. What is needed is more attention on promoting the knowledge-enabling capabilities of new technology investments and less on trying to promote the virtues of KM to people who fail to understand either KM itself or its importance to what they do in their day-to-day working lives. Technology is giving KM its greatest opportunity to shine and yet some KM practitioners seem unable to grasp the simplicity of the situation. I believe the maxim "don't look a gift-horse in the mouth" neatly sums it up.

Most managers believe that they need to invest in expensive new technologies to support KM work in their organizations. This is a false assumption. With a little fine-tuning and imagination, many IT systems can be used by KM practitioners, especially virtual communities, to facilitate KM practices. Even the ubiquitous e-mail has the capacity to become a community host. In fact, most major e-mail solutions, such as Microsoft's Outlook or IBM's Lotus eMail, have the functionality to support the basic needs of collaborative communities. Of course, many KM practitioners will need more sophisticated functionality and systems, but at the very least, customizing an e-mail system will enable every organization to get into the KM game.

The crucial lesson to be learned here is that enabling individuals and communities with the means to share and re-use knowledge is the surest way to move the organizational KM yardsticks forward—and it does not need to come with a large price-tag.

LESSON 8: IT DOES MATTER WHAT YOU CALL IT

One of the enduring issues for those working in the field of KM is what to call it. This may sound a little too esoteric an argument for some, but the truth is that this can have a profound impact on both how you position KM work in your organization, and on its subsequent chances of being a success. For whatever reason, the term *KM* is not being wholeheartedly embraced by senior mangers and organizational planners. In fact, I have been amazed over the last few years to find the lengths to which some practitioners have gone to disguise the fact that they are doing KM at all, often using other terms to describe the work they do. If actual KM practitioners are being forced to adopt this approach, it tells you that they do not have any faith in the marketability of the term *KM*, and that they are seeing it as a potential liability as they try to embed the organizational changes necessary to move the management of knowledge forward. I have found over the course of a number of years that this is probably the reality.

Much as the initial reaction to this issue is to think, "what's in a name?" It appears that the answer is, "Quite a lot." If you want to have any chance of a successful outcome for a KM initiative, it is vital to conduct a successful marketing campaign around it. What you actually call it is, to some extent, irrelevant. The best approach is to latch onto a strategic organizational objective and use a label for KM in the context of that objective. At PWGSC, we ended up using the term *knowledge mobilization*. This worked on several levels: First, it was aligned in terms of the most senior managers' accountability accord; second, it is a very proactive and descriptive label, one that seems to imply something dynamic and worthwhile; and last, it kept the initials of KM intact and thus was more acceptable to the true die-hard practitioners in the organization.

Whatever label you select, it is equally important to have a compelling storyline in terms of a marketing plan. The plan needs to be smart enough to address business-level concerns about activities, possible resource implications, and other organizational impacts and still vague enough to allow for some wiggle room as things unfold. From my perspective, vague can be a major selling point, although you would probably never use that term in front of business managers or at the senior-management table. What you are actually selling is a dynamic of flexibility and responsiveness and, if packaged in that way, vague can be a winner.

So, here is an overview of a good, successful approach to marketing KM in an organization. It is based upon a three-tiered strategic framework. The first tier addresses the organization's basic knowledge needs including activities such as problem solving, business-activity knowledge requirements, customer relationship management, and IM practices. The second tier addresses the organization's enabling knowledge needs including business processes, business intelligence, content integration, sharing and reuse activity, and dependency identification. The third tier addresses the organization's strategic knowledge needs including promoting teams, networks and communities, and evolution toward becoming a learning organization.

Each of these three tiers has accompanying tasks and measures that address the objectives, audience, strategies, competencies, issues, critical success factors, and, most important, the role of KM in facilitating each outcome. This framework of tasks, dependencies, and outcomes will provide a solid platform for any marketing activity.

The crucial lesson to be learned here is that knowledge managers need to become entrepreneurs and learn how to sell the concept of KM before they attempt to engage the organization in embracing the practices of KM.

In conclusion, remember that lessons learned and best practices are no more than a collection of experiences captured in the context of how, when, and where they were learned or applied. They are not an infallible set of instructions you have to follow. Use lessons learned to your advantage, but do not rely on them to be an exact template for how you should proceed. Most of all, be aware that lessons learned can just as easily become impediments to your progress, forming invisible but potentially powerful barriers to further learning and innovation.

TAKE-AWAY MENU

Here are five things worth remembering about *lessons learned*:

I.   Lessons learned have value in highlighting the possible successes and pitfalls that may await you, but they are not a blueprint for success, only an indicator of what you may need to pay special attention to when trying to resolve knowledge-based problems in your organization.

2. Lessons learned are only useful to you if you understand the context in which they were captured.

3. Make sure that you not only plan to capture lessons learned in your organization, but that you plan for the implementation of feedback mechanisms that tie those lessons to some practical uses for future work.

4. The lessons around human behavior are the most useful indicators for assessing potential problems that may lie ahead on the way to implementing KM.

5. Look to see who in the organization might also be able to learn from your KM lessons, especially where inter-dependencies are clearly recognized, such as with the IT or human resources areas.

EIGHT

Successful Knowledge Management

Case Studies from the Public Sector

I particularly like this quote of Churchill's, not so much because
I believe it is necessary to have multiple failures in order to reach
success, but rather because I believe that without a level of enthusiasm you can't expect to change anything in life. Business change
is difficult enough to effect at any time, but especially so where
KM is involved, given the current lack of support from the corporate sector for any work in the knowledge domain. But, before
we get too overwhelmed by the issues and obstacles that stand in
our way, let us take some time to consider a few of the many
successful KM initiatives under way in public sectors around
the world. The case studies included here all have elements of

stealth about them, and all were designed with the intent of leading organizations to new ways of thinking and working. Each of
these initiatives took a different approach to engendering change
in their organizations: through the use of technology tools or
through the restructuring of business processes and approaches.
In the case of the United Kingdom (UK) government's Working
Without Walls initiative, organizations themselves are actually
being physically restructured. Each case study section contains
a summary of the initiative, a list of lessons learned, and a
take-away menu of key issues and opportunities to consider.
Remember that all the planning and talking on KM is only there
to serve one purpose—the actually doing of KM—and these case
studies allow us to see how some public sector organizations have
gone about actually doing KM. As Karl-Erik Sveiby (1997) states
in *The New Organizational Wealth,* "the only valuable knowledge is that
which equips us for action and that kind of knowledge is learned
the hard way—by doing" (p. 202).

These case studies come from a number of different con-
tinents and public sectors, and are all examples of how KM
attributes can flourish in any organization given the right set of
circumstances and a bit of luck. While the mention of luck may
seem a non sequitur to some, it remains a factor in any successful
endeavor. There is just no way to predict luck, so the best thing
to do is prepare a contingency plan in case, and hope it never
has to be implemented.

What these studies all have in common is that they are solutions crafted in direct response to a pressing business issue. Some
business issues might be internal in nature, how to retain corporate knowledge for example, some might be external in nature,
how to maximize customer learning for example, but in all cases
these issues were perceived as being business problems, not KM
problems. This is significant, as the organizational perception
of what is, or is not, a problem needs to drive all solutions,
particularly so in the case of KM. What I mean by this is that too

often KM practitioners approach the business organization with a solution looking for a problem, and not, as it should be, the other way round. If KM has been well marketed, and properly aligned, in the organization (see Chapters 3 and 4) it is far more likely that business owners will come looking for a solution from the KM community. This is the only sure recipe for a stable and defendable rationale for using KM tools and techniques in response to business pressures. The maxim of "build it and they will come" just does not ring true if you look at the mass of evidence from KM initiatives that have failed. In fact, the first case study highlights this exact issue as the FAA initially failed in its attempt to install a KM technology, but then quickly learnt the lessons of failure and adapted their approach to ensure that KM found its proper level in their business community.

Case Study 1: The Federal Aviation Administration, Washington, DC—As Stealthy as It Gets

The Federal Aviation Administration (FAA) is responsible for the safety of civil aviation in the United States. The Federal Aviation Act of 1958 created the agency, under the name Federal Aviation Agency, and in 1967 the name was changed to its present form. Headquartered in Washington, DC, the FAA's major roles include the following:

- Regulating civil aviation to promote safety;
- Encouraging and developing civil aeronautics, including new aviation technology;
- Developing and operating a system of air traffic control and navigation for both civil and military aircraft;
- Researching and developing the National Airspace System and civil aeronautics;

- Developing and carrying out programs to control aircraft noise and other environmental effects of civil aviation; and
- Regulating U.S. commercial space transportation.

What Was the Problem?

This is a story of the requirement to find a way to make FAA's business processes more efficient, and the entrepreneurial way that two employees ensured that KM was successfully used in the search for a solution to the problem. The KM solution that FAA has now implemented is called the *KSN*, the knowledge services network, and it is the brainchild of two entrepreneurial souls—Ron Simmons and Robert Turner. Simmons is the FAA's scientific and technical advisor, and it was he who was challenged in 1995 by the then chief scientist for human factors to find a way to make FAA's business processes more efficient.

What Was the Response to the Problem?

Stage 1: Some Painful Lessons to Be Learned (1996–1998)

The first thing that FAA decided to do was to install some collaborative software technology solutions in response to this challenge. This was a classic case of "build it, and they will *not* come," as a technical team installed a technology solution without there being any dialogue with the business users about what their preferences or suggestions for possible approaches might be. Inevitably the technology-first approach hit a brick wall, and Ron and his team came to the conclusion that finding out more about collaborative processes might actually have been a better place to start. So Ron immersed himself in a study on collaborative work practices, and then wrote a paper on this for distribution across FAA.

Stage 2: If at First You Do Not Succeed. . . . (1999–2000)

Once the lessons from stage 1 had been absorbed, it was decided to retry establishing a collaborative technology solution. A new technology was selected, and this time the business community was included in the planning and design of the solution from day one. The result was a limited deployment (around 50 users) of a technology solution known as KMS2000. This collaborative environment was a success, although limited in its scope, and the software solution itself won an award in a Microsoft-sponsored competition.

Stage 3: The Evolution of the KSN (2001–2004)

Ron realized that if he was to take collaboration to the next level, he needed to build a proper framework for KM deployment at FAA. Accordingly, he sought help from the George Washington University (GWU) KM business program to help him design such a framework based on GWU's KM business model, the "four pillars" as it is called. This model incorporating people, process, technology, and training has formed the basis of FAA's KM program since 2001. In particular, Ron was keen to see a robust training module evolve along with the KM program, as this was seen as being a critical factor for a successful deployment of the technology.

Once the four foundation pieces of the KM framework were ready, FAA ran a pilot study of a user group that was willing to trial the framework concepts against a technology they already had installed as a collaborative platform. The pilot proved to be an invaluable testing ground for proving concepts and gauging business-users' willingness to take on board KM disciplines and techniques. Especially significant during the pilot was the way that key design components were created and validated. In particular the following components had long-term significance for the successful implementation of the KSN:

- The core design team concept: Individuals responsible from across the organization for the design and evolution of each of the four KM framework pillars: people, technology, process, and learning.
- The concept of using facilitators and the recognition of the need for the provision of facilitator training.
- The use of a human factors research approach to gauging business performance and to identifying and defining business trends.
- An understanding of the need for an organizational convergence of KM, virtual work, and learning.

Once the pilot was concluded in March of 2002, Ron Simmons joined forces with another FAA KM advocate, Robert Turner, the founder of the FAA's Team Technology Center, to implement the concept of the KSN. Between them they selected a technology platform, designed the business rules around its deployment, and created a number of tools and processes for use by FAA's business community, these included the following:

- A rapid prototyping approach to KSN deployment in support of business objectives.
- A broad guidance aimed at establishing stability and governance for the overall KM program, while also encouraging a concept of self-ownership in which the network comprises various self-governed communities, or nodes, which have autonomy in the design and operation of their specific programs.
- A KM program risk model, designed to establish a balance of the four KM pillars, for use by business units. The concept is that a balanced KM program will divide its emphasis as follows: 30 percent people, 30 percent

technology, 20 percent processes, and 20 percent training.

- A tracking and review mechanism to ensure KSN communities (nodes) remain relevant and purposeful. The review of performance statistics is used to decide when intervention by the KSN general manager is needed to either reenergize the community or declare it moribund and in need of removal from the KSN.

One of the most significant aspects of the KSN deployment is that it was achieved at all, given the lack of endorsement by the organizations technology group. The central technology unit does not actually support KSN's technology platform, it endorses and supports an entirely different technology base. This means that people power is much in evidence here. Not only was the technology chosen outside of the auspices of the central information technology (IT) group, it was also initially deployed and supported from within the KSN community itself. I do not believe that it this is a situation that occurs very often in large organizations, but it is interesting to be able to confirm that often stealth is a more important success factor than political correctness. In fact as the KSN has now moved from being a low-exposure pilot opportunity to a full-fledged production-type environment, it is obvious that a repatriation of the support function back to the central technology group will probably be necessary sooner or later.

What Was the Outcome of the Response?

As the FAA is conducting one of the largest innovation activities in the federal government, the creation of the next generation of national airspace system (NAS) technology, the overarching purpose of the KSN was to meet user's business process needs and to do it in a way that increased innovative capacity.

The initial deployment of the KSN involved two business units and approximately 50 users. Over a 3-year span that number has dramatically increased to more than 160 business units and more than 16,000 users, including many senior managers within FAA, FAA regional users throughout the United States, and many external stakeholders such as national and regional airlines, airline unions, the National Aeronautics and Space Administration (NASA), and many others in the general aviation community.

Some core business areas now supported by KSN includes the following:

- The Operations Center that provides command and control communications functions for crisis response teams.
- The Associate Administrators group that reviews major air transportation capacity issues.
- The team responsible for management and acquisition of major systems for use in the National Airspace System.
- Terminal Area Operations Aviation Committee (TAOARC), the committee responsible for creating regulations to make airports safer.

At the same time, FAA has put together a number of indicators, divided into qualitative and quantitative groupings, to help assess the business value of the KSN and to describe its activities, although not all of the indicators are currently being measured due to time and resource constraints. The current qualitative indicators are facilitator surveys, impact on public, quality of crisis responses, quality of rulemaking, and user response. The current quantitative indicators are: dollars saved, time saved, usage statistics, manager participation, process efficiency, and desired behaviors.

Take-Aways

Here are some of the lessons and value-add components that have emerged from the deployment of the KSN:

1. An understanding that a successful knowledge management program depends on integrating people, processes, technology, and learning—the four pillars of the current system.
2. The validation of the core design team concept.
3. First-hand experience of the benefits of working closely with business managers.
4. The concept of facilitator and facilitator training.
5. A human factors research approach to gauging performance and defining trends.
6. An understanding of the convergence of knowledge management, virtual work, and learning.

At the same time, a number of key roles evolved necessary for the successful deployment and management of the KSN. These were:

The sponsor: A champion for the KSN, who had access to the senior leadership, but who was not associated with a specific business line. In FAA this is the manager for internal communications. This choice was also directed by the example of America On Line (AOL), where the champion for AOL's equivalent of the KSN is also the internal communications manager.

The General manager: The overall leader of the KSN community, responsible for maintenance of the software, training of facilitators, acquisition of needed resources, and coordination of the community.

Nodes: This is the descriptor FAA gives to the communities that use the KSN. All nodes attach to preexisting FAA offices, thus ensuring that KSN works intuitively within the organizational hierarchy, not against it.

Node administrators: Usually a business manager who is responsible for ensuring the node remains functional.

Node facilitators: The people who provide the critical day-to-day support for KSN users. They also relay ideas for KSN adaptation and growth to the general manager and the strategic planning team. The facilitators are given 2 days of initial training, which includes an introduction to knowledge-sharing principles and technical training.

Technical support: People with technical proficiency are distributed throughout the KSN—the most successful nodes almost all have a tight administrator–technologist partnership. This allows real-time or near–real-time adjustments to the system. In one instance the business leader and the technologist are the same person.

Government responsible individual (GRI): The GRI for each node is responsible for maintaining government control of the platform and ensuring that appropriate norms and procedures are followed for the use of a government resource.

The KSN Planning Group: Drawn from across the business, this is a small group (seven people) who provide strategic planning and oversight for the KSN.

Finally, and perhaps even more important than the specific roles within the KSN community is the people-centric philosophy that drives the existence of the environment: The KSN is first and foremost a community of people working together and sharing knowledge. Accordingly, the growth and propagation of the network is strictly a people-to-people dynamic, taking advantage of the existing connections within the organization. All the other pillars of the program, process, technology, and learning revolve around people and take into consideration priorities in their work. The design of the network, both formal and informal, acknowledges the need for individuals to become comfortable with the principles of KM before attempting to utilize the network.

In Summary

The FAA case study is instructive in showing that not all KM initiatives need to have a grand design, or even targeted outcomes, to be successful. Most organizations like to plan thoroughly and prepare their business programs through a well-structured and formalized methodology. KM does not always need such thorough preparation, in fact it appears that many successful KM deployments are pretty much unstructured and seem to be implemented successfully despite the organization's best efforts to keep them under corporate controls and guidelines. In the case of FAA, it appears that two strong individuals understood the organization's KM needs and constructed a solution to those needs that literally worked its way through the organization from the ground up. While this KM tool has been accepted by the organization as a whole and has senior management backing, it is worth remembering that to properly deploy and maintain it in the years to come, the organization's IT group will need to play a major role. I think the message is clear, go ahead and work on KM solutions from the grass-roots perspective, but do not alienate any other parts of the organization, especially the IT folks, in the process, as they may hold the keys to the long-term success and viability of any KM initiative.

CASE STUDY 2: THE UK GOVERNMENT'S KM NATIONAL PROJECT—KNOWLEDGE MANAGEMENT FINDS ITS PLACE IN THE E-GOVERNMENT WORLD

This case study is one that opens up a whole new world of possibility for the application of KM in a government context.

The UK Government's KM National Project was established by the Office of the Deputy Prime Minister in partnership with the Improvement and Development Agency (IDeA), and launched as a local e-government national project in October of 2004. The project's vision is to achieve a consistent KM system in place across all local authorities. IDeA was created by and for local government in England and Wales and is independent of central government and regulatory bodies. It is accountable to local government through a Board of Directors, half of whom are local government councilors, and its mandate is to stimulate and support continual and self-sustaining improvement and development within local government.

The KM National Project is being delivered through a series of best practice work streams developed by local authority partnerships and led by Wiltshire County Council. The aims of the project are to:

- Carry out a national exploration of the role of knowledge management and its potential impact on public policy.
- Identify the organizational and sectoral relationships that are necessary to underpin effective knowledge management systems.
- Help identify a process for developing legal protocols.
- Incorporate opportunities for developing the potential for greater learning and mutual problem-solving both with the community and community leaders.
- Develop technical products that offer an acceptable single point of access and can 'hold' complex layers of information.

What Was the Problem?

The problem facing local government in the UK was that while many local authority organizations were looking at, and even implementing, KM systems, tools, and techniques, the various proposed solutions were being developed and implemented in isolation to other local authorities. In fact there was no effective and consistent knowledge management system that could be implemented across the full range of local authorities. The challenge was to develop a fully comprehensive range of toolkits and processes, which every local authority would be able to understand and access. To do so would require the development and implementation of a number of KM work streams that could be linked together to deliver products that would:

- Improve democratic accountability.
- Increase the number of well-informed community leaders.
- Raise public service standards.
- Empower communities.

The project team recognized that three main challenges would need to be resolved if local authority organizations were to reach the state of fully effective information and data sharing, and the re-using of knowledge to maximum benefit. These challenges were as follows:

- How to correctly describe the knowledge so that it will appear to have benefit to organizations and communities.
- How to develop a culture within an organization that not only encourages the sharing of information but also encourages people to seek advice and assistance from others outside of their own immediate environments.
- What systems, both electronic and human, need to be put in place in order to ensure creation, efficient flow and distribution of knowledge?

Within this context, the efficient management of knowledge resources was seen as a key issue in enabling local authorities to work more effectively in delivering the broad range of services they provide to their local communities, and in enabling them to provide opportunities for more interactions between the information, consultation, access to community, professional and business networks, they deal with.

What Was the Response to the Problem?

First the project team decided to set a proper context for the work ahead and provided a definition of KM that it was hoped would facilitate a common understanding of what KM meant and more important, how it would facilitate the objectives of the project. The project team used the working definition of KM:

> *The creation and subsequent management of an environment that encourages knowledge to be created, shared, learnt, enhanced, organized and exploited for the benefit of the organization and its customers.*

The information and skills held within the local authority organizations were seen as being central to their achieving key targets and objectives and in ensuring positive collaboration and strengthening relationships among employees and partners. Therefore, to be most effective, this locally held knowledge would need to be easily accessed, shared, and combined to provide maximum benefit to those who needed it. However, identifying the multiple sources of information and establishing common platforms and a central data bank would be a difficult task in an environment as diverse as a local authority. Add in the complexity of a new business model evolving around the requirement to deliver services online, and you have quite a challenge to meet.

It was decided that the KM National Project would therefore focus on providing a series of individual solution sets that could at the same time be interlinked to form a holistic approach to solving the problem. These solution sets are provided through a number of work streams, seven in all, covering the following dimensions:

1. A KM Roadmap
2. Local Intelligence Systems and Information Asset Registers
3. CPA (Comprehensive Performance Assessment) Improvement and Planning
4. Customer-Facing Programs
5. Tacit Knowledge
6. Proof of Concept: Strengthening Communities in Rural Areas
7. Community Knowledge in Policy Development

It is intended that the work streams will provide the opportunity to test, develop, and replicate processes for the following:

- Joining up and building trust between organizations, services and councilors.
- Information security.
- Establishing legal frameworks.
- Building one-stop-shop information websites.
- Supporting community leaders

Each work stream is being led by local authorities, either individually or in partnership with other authorities. They are going to be the *guinea pigs* who will try out the proposed tools and techniques within each stream, assess their effectiveness, and provide a feedback loop to the project for refinement of the various approaches before they are applied in a more general setting. The aim of the work stream projects is to deliver the following benefits:

- Well-informed community leaders providing easily accessible and well-organized information about their localities.
- Empowered communities with a comprehensive range of accessible local knowledge, thus enhancing local participation in community issues.
- Strong local e-Democracies with local councilors and local communities having easy access to information on consultation outcomes.
- Increased service standards with councils and other agencies sharing information for maximum collaborative advantage.

Work Stream 1: A Knowledge Management Roadmap.
(London Borough of Camden)

The KM Roadmap was developed to provide local authorities with the means to effect the transition from *information management* to *knowledge management* and to benefit from the organizational and financial effectiveness and efficiencies this can bring. Drawing on the practices and experiences of specialists in the public, private and academic fields, the Roadmap provides an overview of the use of knowledge management within a local authority context and the key factors, issues, opportunities and constraints to be considered when developing and implementing a knowledge management culture and systems. The Roadmap enables local authorities to benchmark "where are we now?" and provides informed and practical guidance on "how do we get there?" building on existing initiatives and processes, within a national standards framework to integrate with other National Projects and ultimately create *knowledge organizations*. The Web-based self-assessment system enables local authorities to plot their strengths and weaknesses against the four cornerstones of the knowledge management process and to gauge the specific needs of their organization. Steps to achieving the transition goals through practical application and focus within a number of key components are then recommended. The four cornerstones are as follows:

- Information management
- Customer focus
- Communications
- Organizational learning

The Roadmap further contributes to the creation of local authority *knowledge organizations* by establishing a community of practice of change agents tasked with implementing knowledge management processes within their own organizations. Gathering examples of best practice, delivery challenges, and change management issues, the community of practice will be a valuable pool of resource to inform and assist local authorities in their knowledge management strategies. The Roadmap contains seven areas of focus:

1. Introduction to KM: Focused on those in local authorities who may not be familiar with KM or those who feel they would benefit from a refresher before going on to the main section of the KM Roadmap itself.
2. Information management in KM: Describes ways that the use of information can enable the local authority achieve its immediate targets and create both organizational and policy improvements.
3. Customer focus: Looks at how KM techniques can be used to improve service planning and give an organization a better customer focus.

4.   Communications: Looks at how good communications can help target and customize the relevant information and knowledge that employees need to help them do their job better.

5.   Organizational learning: Looks at ways to ensure the learning's from people doing their daily job are transferred to others who need it.

6.   Implementing the KM Roadmap: Provides simple, easy to follow, and practical advice on the stages needed to become a learning organization.

7.   Supporting Communities of Practice (CoP) in local authorities: Supports the deployment of CoP through the provision of best practice information, CoP case studies, and software designed by the project team to facilitate the maintenance of a CoP.

Work Stream 2: Local Intelligence Systems and Information Asset Registers (Wiltshire County Council)

The project has developed toolkits to help local authorities develop local intelligence systems and/or information asset registers that provide relevant, current and accessible knowledge to create user-friendly local intelligence to inform decision making. These are aimed at facilitating the effective management of information flows within the authority itself and between the authority and its citizens. As not all information is relevant to all areas, there is still a need to identify what information is relevant and how it can best be stored, accessed, and used to maximum effect. The KM local intelligence systems and information asset registers are intended to address the issues surrounding the capture, storing and accessing of relevant information that can be made available to the local authority, its partners and its citizens. The objective is to inform and empower the local authority and the community it serves.

The local intelligence systems tool kit was been developed as a resource for those responsible for developing information stores within their organization. Based on examples of best practice and tested within six pilot authorities, the tool kit provides advice on how best to integrate current systems within a standard framework to harness the information available and maximize its value.

The information asset register tool kit was developed to help local authorities summarize their information assets, and point to where they are held. It is aimed at those responsible for information management within their organization and those involved in promoting openness and information sharing across an authority or partnership, perhaps in a Freedom of Information context.

The toolkit gives practical *how to* guidance on developing sound and efficient processes, reducing the requirement for initial systems and requirements, and promoting good practice by reference to current practice and sources to encourage consistency of approach and adoption of common standards. Its objective is to provide a mechanism for consistent and structured information management, which will aid research projects, information reviews, audits, working parties, e-government planning and business process re-engineering. It can also assist information openness, with particular reference to compliance with the UKs Freedom of Information Act and the European Union's Directive on the Re-use of Public Sector Information.

Work Stream 3: CPA Improvement and Planning (Birmingham City Council)

The Local Government White Paper, Strong Local Leadership Quality Public Services tasked the UK's Audit Commission with carrying out Comprehensive Performance Assessments (CPAs) for councils in England. These assessments are aimed at evaluating the delivery of core services, and the corporate strength of each local council, through information drawn from a range of government inspector's reports, performance indicators, audits, and assessments of service plans. The CPA process is seen as the main tool for identifying poor performance and the principle starting point to assess the need for central government support or intervention.

This work stream is focused on showing how KM is relevant to public sector personnel and the ways in which it can help improve the quality of basic services. In response to CPA factors such as changed public perception of the quality of the services they are being provided, the effective use of KM approaches and techniques offers authorities a way both to make full use of the assets they already have and to develop the new ones they need to meet future challenges. Accordingly, the KM for Service Improvement project provides two *cookbooks* that offer local authorities a way into exploring the use of KM for improving services and responding to the demands of CPA.

The first of these cookbooks brings together the basic information needed to understand the importance of KM for service improvement. To achieve this, it draws on a number of sources of information about what KM is and how it supports innovation and improvement work generally. The main part of this guide is taken up with describing a number of basic tools and techniques which can be used by almost every authority. Most of these techniques do not need Information Communications Technology (ICT) systems to be used and most of them can be used in small sections as well as across an entire council. The first cookbook also includes some basic guidance on the use of ICT and the applicability of frameworks and some advice on producing corporate frameworks, strategies, and business cases. It also provides links to more detailed academic treatment of most of the major topics for those who would like to explore these in more detail.

The second Cookbook consists of a small collection of case studies that provide more detailed examples of using KM to improve services. They are reasonably short and accessible, and most of them were written by local government employees. The second cookbook also includes a short commentary and two-way links to the appropriate sections of the guidance cookbook.

Work Stream 4: Customer-Facing Program (London Borough of Tower Hamlets)

The focus of the KM Customer-Facing Program is to help bring *back office* information to *front-line* customer-facing employees in a quick and user friendly format. It was developed to help local authorities face the challenge of sharing and transferring information and skill from the *back* to the *front* by creating electronic content for mediated services through the use of a series of templates designed to ensure a flow of knowledge can be channeled to those who need it most. Based on examples of best practice within local authorities, the templates contain information to support employees in their front-line dealings with the public to ensure effective and efficient delivery. With content organized by service type for easy search and reference, the templates provide users with information on how best to complete tasks that apply to that particular service and should result in faster more efficient and consistent service delivery by better informed employees. Although generic so they can be used by all local authorities, the templates have been created in a style that allows local customization in line with guidelines developed in partnership with the Local Authority Web sites (LAWS) National Project.

Support to local authorities is provided via documentation and a user forum where employees can share and build on each others' experiences and expertise. The templates can also be extended and developed as further mediated and other services are identified that could be supported in this format.

Work Stream 5: Tacit Knowledge (London Borough of Lewisham)

Local authorities, in common with all organizations, are challenged with delivering services or products in the most effective and efficient way. The central factor to achieving these aims is making the best use of the information and skills that are held within: the organizational knowledge that relates to personal experiences, tips, contacts, insights, and judgments that even the individual is often unaware of. Accordingly, the Tacit Knowledge project is focused on developing ways of capturing this hidden knowledge and in creating knowledge sharing cultures that can find and access this knowledge in the quickest, most effective and most cost-efficient way. The project is looking to help local authorities identify ways of capturing unique tacit knowledge and making it explicit so that it is available to be shared, used, and built on by the organization to improve its service delivery.

Based on current local authority information management standards and examples of best practice within the public, private, and academic fields, the project has developed a generic architecture for the capture of tacit knowledge and the recording, storing, sharing, and accessing explicit knowledge through the use of defined *meta-data,* or information labeling standards and techniques such as *blogging* or *Web-logging*. Best practice guidelines have also been developed on implementing accessible and effective directory services.

However, such techniques can only be effective if the right environment exists. To assist local authorities in developing the necessary "knowledge sharing culture," a human resources tool kit has been created that provides information and advice on encouraging volunteering of tacit knowledge through techniques, culture change, and establishing communities of practice and knowledge networks both within the organization and across its partners and citizens.

With the study of tacit knowledge capture in its infancy, a community of practice has also been established to test developing techniques, gather case studies of best practice, and provide a forum for the exchange of information, ideas, and experience to the benefit of all local authorities.

Work Stream 6: Strengthening Communities in Rural Areas
(Wiltshire County Council)

Local authorities in rural areas need to understand their communities to ensure relevant and practical policy decision making. To develop and deliver the most appropriate services to their community, local authorities need to gather the most up-to-date information available from a range of partners, agencies, groups, and citizens. Once gathered, this information has to be stored to allow quick, efficient, and economical access when needed. Such a process can prove challenging for urban authorities even with a wealth of information at their fingertips and is an even greater challenge for rural authorities where remoteness and isolation issues often render efficient two-way communication difficult.

The KM Strengthening Communities in Rural Areas project builds on the work developed by the Local Intelligence Systems (LIS) project to deliver a proof of concept specifically focused on strategies and methods for collecting and displaying rural intelligence.

Based on examples of best practice, current levels, and availability of information and rural local authority requirements, the rural intelligence tool kit provides an overview of the need for rural intelligence at a local level, analysis of key policies and research on the subject, LIS planning guidelines, and listings of the key data sources for rural LIS development.

The rural intelligence tool kit provides the opportunity to improve decision making and service delivery within remote communities by gathering information and intelligence to build a full picture of local characteristics and trends in rural areas. The additional use of geographical information system (GIS) technology enhances the ability of local authorities and partner organizations to map and overlay their data at a local level to improve profiling, monitoring and evaluation of the impact of policies and initiatives.

The aim of the project is to show that a comprehensive and user-friendly LIS can deliver significant benefits to areas of data collection, consultation, policy decision making, and service delivery within a rural local authority by providing readily accessible knowledge to inform and influence decisions.

Work Stream 7: Community Knowledge in Policy Development (Leeds and Newcastle City Councils)

To develop policies and services that best meet the needs of their communities and citizens, local authorities need to engage with and involve these groups and individuals in their decision making processes. To do this successfully it is necessary first to identify ways in which stakeholders may be more involved in developing policy, and second to develop methods of accessing the knowledge that exists within the community to improve the relevance of these policies. The KM Community Knowledge in Policy Development project was established to identify examples of best practice and build a common framework for community engagement with policy development. The creation of this community knowledge in policy development tool kit will enable local authorities to consult the relevant knowledge holders within their community on areas of policy development that are relevant to them.

Given the number and variety of groups and individuals who could be considered for inclusion in policy development, particular focus was placed on the multiagency Local Strategic

Partnerships, with which local authorities work and operate within. To ensure that stakeholders are involved in consultation only on policy topics that are relevant to their particular area of interest, a record of these areas of interest and the preferred method of communication, for example via the internet or SMS messaging, is captured. A *classification and matching engine* was also developed to categorize and sort these records of interest.

In Summary

Although it is too early to be able to assess the results of the seven work streams contained in the UK's KM National Project, it is apparent that this project is a significant milestone in the use of KM tools and techniques in a public sector environment. It may be an ambitious undertaking given its scope, but it is well thought out and seeks to address all the fundamental building blocks necessary to be in place for KM to succeed at an enterprise level: human resource issues; effective decision-making issues; analysis and planning issues; knowledge identification, sharing, and reuse issues; improved business process and service delivery issues; communication issues; organizational learning issues; information management in KM issues; implementation issues; community development and support issues; and technology issues. All in all, a pretty comprehensive attempt at addressing KM implementation in a public sector environment.

Case Study 3: The Australian Bureau of Statistics—Keeping it Simple

The Australian Bureau of Statistics (ABS) is Australia's national statistical agency. Its mission is to assist and encourage informed decision making, research and discussion within governments and the community. The agency is also one of Australia's largest publishers with hundreds of titles in print, and a Web site containing close to 300,000 pages of content. The ABS has been consistently ranked among the top two in the world in terms of statistical agencies.

ABS as an organization has stated its commitment to encouraging innovation, intelligent risk taking, and adaptability to change in its employees and to creating a culture that fosters communication, information sharing, and teamwork between all levels, offices, and workgroups. In fact ABS' corporate plan includes the following objectives for its staff:

> *Utilizing our comparative advantage in access to knowledge and a world class technology environment by: Improving the ways we capture, share, organize and access knowledge and expertise; and, Exploiting technologies as enablers of innovation, productivity and excellence.*

What Was the Problem?

Although ABS has continually sought to foster a collaborative environment, one where knowledge and information sharing is the norm, they realized that there needed to be a knowledge strategy, based on the use of a technology tool, that allowed the ongoing management of the organization's knowledge assets.

What Was the Response to the Problem?

Stage 1: Putting the Infrastructure in Place (1993–2000)

From the beginning, ABS has been focused on how to lever its technology investments to achieve its corporate knowledge management goals and objectives. However, ABS believes that the first component of implementing a technology solution successfully is preparing the workforce in terms of its business rules and processes. Accordingly, the organization has worked extensively over the years to foster a culture that is supportive of KM concepts and practices. ABS staff tends to have long and diverse careers, and they appreciate the benefits that come from documenting and sharing. Those who move around an organization tend to appreciate the value of a good knowledge base, one which helps them feel more comfortable in a new role, and so ABS employees are encouraged to leave a similar legacy for their successor. Also, ABS promotes a collaborative and noncompetitive approach to work, and makes extensive use of multi-disciplined teams. The emphasis is very much on adopting a corporate approach, and this means that individuals and workgroups are usually more than willing to share their information and knowledge with others.

ABS believes that it is entirely logical for it to install a KM infrastructure as most of its staff is knowledge workers, and giving them the tools to manage their knowledge will make the organization more productive. In ABS, both KM and IM have a long association with technology, and the organization's early trials of network and remote-access technology allowed it to evaluate the way that its employees and technology interact. This was particularly important in establishing a value-proposition with management for the way that technology could support innovation, creativity and new approaches in the workplace. It is also worth noting that ABS does not waste its time debating definitions of KM, but rather follows the dialogues and outcomes from the world KM community, with the intent of utilizing good ideas and successful KM approaches in its own KM environment.

In 1993, ABS decided to implement a technology that would facilitate the management of information and knowledge assets, and at the same time meet the requirements of workgroups and communities for a collaborative desktop environment. In conjunction with the technical rollout, ABS decided to adopt an explicit knowledge strategy, which they called the *object management strategy*—the intention being to emphasize the need to manage both the object (of any type) and the information (meta-data) that described it. The object management strategy also incorporated a simple knowledge framework and identified the cultural and technical elements that the senior management believed were necessary to successfully foster a work environment characterized by communication, collaboration, automated workflow, effective resource discovery, and the transfer of knowledge. The intention behind the strategy was to specifically identify the extent to which the technology environment might be an enabler for the corporate goal of better knowledge management.

The initial knowledge framework that ABS implemented was intended to allow employees to more easily categorize and manage knowledge and information. At the same time, a major consideration for ABS, as it is with most public-sector organizations, was the need to manage their records. Therefore it was decided that all knowledge and information within the organization would fall into one of three categories: corporate, workgroup, or personal. All work, communications, and knowledge and information components are considered to have been produced or undertaken in one of these three domains. ABS encourages employees to work in only two of the domains, corporate or workgroup, and by so doing believe that organizational knowledge and information can be properly discovered, managed, and shared as a corporate asset.

At the same time as they implemented the knowledge framework, ABS specifically targeted supporting work in the corporate and workgroup domains through the use of enabling tools and knowledge-based work practices and processes. Tools that were developed to support work at the personal level specifically incorporated features that facilitated transfer to the corporate or workgroup environments. An outcome of this approach is that ABS meets its recordkeeping obligations by simply managing the content in the corporate and workgroup environment, ignoring content in the personal domain.

Stage 2: Putting More Emphasis on Knowledge (2000–2004)

Although the object management strategy (OMS) was successful in changing the way that ABS managed its knowledge and information sources, it became apparent that a more robust knowledge framework was required to meet the increasing emphasis being placed on knowledge management within the bureau. Accordingly, a decision was made to update the OMS with a new knowledge strategy aimed at facilitating a more knowledgeable way of working. The most important feature of the 2000 strategy was the development of a set of specific organizational information behaviors that were aimed at fostering the development of a sharing philosophy in the bureau. These behaviors are seen as so important from a business perspective, that all employees are introduced to them as Lesson 1 in the ABS's *Introduction to the Desktop* (desktop fundamentals) course.

Information behaviors support the knowledge framework through a set of personal, workgroup, and corporate KM practices that encourage staff to create information that can be used and shared. These behaviors make explicit the types of workpractices which support knowledgeable working. They include the following:

- Seeking out, reusing, and building on existing knowledge wherever you can
- Working to ensure that you have the skills to efficiently and effectively locate information
- Recognizing that workgroups need to share knowledge
- Playing a part in maintaining workgroup knowledge to facilitate access by others
- Promoting the benefits of information sharing

What Was the Outcome of the Response?

ABS has extracted significant productivity gains from their strategy of exploiting technology and the manner in which people interact with it, and in the promotion of the use of common tools and systems as business process enablers. The bureau has successfully integrated technology into the work of the agency's business, assisting the organization and its people to stay in front rather than behind in meeting the demands for statistical information. To aid this process the agency has standardized on generalized systems in preference to unique systems, and the ABS enterprise architecture, which incorporates the agency's knowledge framework, emphasizes the integration of all ABS' business systems.

ABS has seen that productivity benefits accrue from the reuse of ideas, systems, and processes, and the agency has been prepared to mandate the use of particular tools and techniques. Specifically, the ABS has come to understand the extent to which pervasive use of a toolset across the agency can support the exchange of ideas and promote productivity, innovation, and creativity. This is probably most in evidence in ABS' use of a collaborative desktop platform, with over 1100 applications developed. But the method can also be seen in the agency's approach to data management where extensive work has been devoted to adding and organizing statistical data into input and output data warehouses to create a single publishing source. Underpinning this work at all levels is an extensive understanding of the role that meta-data plays in facilitating the exploitation of resources.

ABS has benefited from the extensive use of workgroup databases which underpin effective approaches to communication, collaboration and information asset management. When ABS originally deployed its OMS technology in 1993 it was decided to promote the use of shared discussion forums as an alternative to e-mail. To emphasize this, the e-mail application was renamed *personal holdings*, to indicate that it was for information that belonged in the *personal* domain. The original application has evolved considerably since 1993, and now contains a range of features, including workgroup-level e-mail developed specifically to support working as part of a group. As a result, ABS now has several hundred workgroup databases—about three times as many as it does defined organizational teams. Effectively, these extra workgroup databases support internal communities of practice and can be seen as working in parallel to the agency's defined organizational structure. By default, workgroups are open access—anyone can search, read, and author documents in other workgroup databases. Another feature of ABS' workgroup databases is the embedding of strong meta-data support for record keeping. When a document is created and assigned a category, it automatically acquires a set of meta-data that controls the access, filing, and life cycle of the document.

To manage its KM initiative, ABS has put together a supporting infrastructure of people and processes, complemented by a KM-focused funding model. A director-level manager ensures coordination of the bureau's knowledge-enabling initiatives, and they are supported by a KM Center of Excellence, which supports, investigates, and delivers services to assist the KM program. Annual funding covers the salaries and the development and configuration of most of the organizations knowledge services and technologies, including learning content and technical developments such as the *Welcome Page* (ABS portal) and the in-house recordkeeping system. More general enabling infrastructure such as the promotion of ABS' sharing philosophy (a cultural KM initiative) is embedded in the organization's induction and learning programs. Many aspects of the core technical infrastructure, such as the organization's workgroup database design template and discovery services, are funded as core infrastructure developments with each rollout of a new release of the collaboration software. In that way, any new KM infrastructure is rolled out as part of core infrastructure changes.

So successful has the KM initiative been, that the Australian Public Service publication, *Embedding the APS Values*, contains a case study on ABS' information sharing approaches.

Stage 3: Managing Process Knowledge (2004—ongoing)

Although the new knowledge strategy has been successful at improving ABS' management of its information assets, it became apparent that there was another management issue still unresolved; that of managing tacit knowledge. As much of the knowledge of how things actually get done still resides in people's heads, the bureau decided it needed to do a better job at managing its process knowledge. In response to that decision, ABS have implemented a new system with the aim of making it much easier to document, operate, understand and modify business processes which are typically a mix of automated and human activities. The key elements of this new system are as follows:

- A corporate library of business processes (in the form of process definitions stored as XML but displayed as flowcharts)
- Services which are invoked by processes (e.g., schedule a meeting or running a computer program for information delivery)
- A workflow engine which carries out the automated parts of a process
- Process control portals which provide the interface for operating, managing and documenting the status of a business process.

The idea behind the process control portal is to incorporate it as a new component of ABS' workgroup databases (WDBs).

By creating and running the processes from the WDBs, the record-keeping infrastructure in the WDBs will automatically be inherited. The hope is that with these components in place, business processes will be as visible and as well managed as any other information asset. ABS has developed a prototype of this system and is planning to deploy it throughout 2005.

Take-Aways

Here are some of the lessons and value-add components that have emerged from the ABS KM initiative:

1. A number of organizational components have to be in place, or put in place, in order to be successful. These include:
   a. An organizational culture that values the sharing of information
   b. A framework that defines the place of all information and knowledge in the organization
   c. A set of information behaviors that encourage the management and sharing of information
   d. Extensive use of knowledge-enabled workplaces
   e. An innovative approach to managing e-mail and electronic record keeping
   f. Sophisticated management of meta-data and its application in business processes

2. You can help change the way that people think about the way they work by empowering them to make decisions about their work. In ABS's case a strong technology foundation played the role of facilitator and allowed employees to influence the way the organization worked through the creation and implementation of new and improved

processes. This change-focused approach throughout the organization has had a positive and beneficial effect on all aspects of work in ABS.

3.   Ownership is a critical success factor. From its beginnings, the ABS KM initiative had strong senior management support and advocates, not just for the technology, but for the organizational work changes it enabled. Accompanying that mindset was strong governance that emphasized the KM model, necessary business commitment, and ownership of the knowledge framework and processes.

In Summary

The ABS case study is a good example of long-term care and planning paying off from a KM perspective. ABS's emphasis on the individual and their knowledge need's was a deliberate and planned strategy, one that is reflected throughout the organization's approach to its work and desired business objectives. ABS seems to have understood the balance that is necessary to achieve between technology and people in any KM initiative. Too often organizations focus on one to the detriment of the other, however ABS recognized very early on the potential benefits of technology, and then worked to educate their workforce about those potential benefits. At the same time they involved employees in the integration of technology solutions into work processes. The result is a working environment that walks the talk, and encourages and empowers employees to share their knowledge and learn from others. All this underpinned by smart technology solutions that align with organizational strategy, and that help individuals and teams to achieve their business objectives and meet their business accountabilities.

Case Study 4: The UK Government—Working Without Walls—Eliminating the Barriers to Knowledge Management

Of all the case studies included here, I find this the most intriguing. Mainly because on the surface this is not a KM initiative at all, and as far as I can tell the term knowledge management does not appear anywhere within the project report that the UK government produced. However, as this case study clearly indicates the transformation of the workplace achieved by this initiative has had two major paybacks: One is the obvious increase in employee satisfaction in regards to their working environment; and the other is the opportunity afforded by these changes for individuals to increase their knowledge sharing practices and opportunities.

What Was the Problem?

In today's economy, knowledge is a growing commodity. It is becoming increasingly important for governments to create working environments that support interaction and collaboration between employees to allow knowledge to be shared, thus helping to break down many of the established hierarchies and silos that inhibit flexibility across teams.

What Was the Response to the Problem?

Increasingly, it is being recognized that the physical workplace can have a significant impact on business efficiency and effectiveness. Put simply, the workplace can support or hinder day-to-day operations, as well as help the process of change and improvement. The impact of the working environment is subtle, but organizations looking to change and improve are beginning to

understand its influence and develop their workplaces to exploit
and maximize business benefits. The need for the modernization
of government is leading to a better focus on business objectives
that also support organizational aspirations around greater efficiency, increased effectiveness, and improved image—mirroring
and evolving developments in the private sector. These visions
are partly being realized by providing the right infrastructure to attract and retain the best people, and by making it
possible for people to work in new and different ways. Successful organizational and business change demands attention to
three elements: people, process, and place. Many believe that
a sense of place has the strongest psychological impact on people and behaviors, allowing it to become a key catalyst for wider
change.

Over the last few years a number of UK government departments have responded to the need for such organizational change
through the refurbishment of their workplaces. A first step in
the change process for all the departments involved has been the
co-location of staff in one building. Bringing staff together in
one location has offered opportunities for increased interaction
and collaboration, particularly at the informal level, as individuals bump into and share information with colleagues previously
located in separate buildings. In fact by co-locating teams,
and improving adjacencies between groups that work closely,
many government organizations are reporting improvements in
corporate information and knowledge exchange.

Also, common to all these initiatives were a number of
concepts being introduced into the new working environment
to better support the diversity of modern working practices and
the needs of the knowledge worker. These concepts include the
following:

Touchdown workbenches—to support short-stay working.
    These are usually placed near entrances or circulation routes

to facilitate the chances of interaction with others and the likelihood of serendipitous meetings of individuals that can promote knowledge exchange.

Team table—to support team working. May be owned by a project or team or used as a work setting for a varying number of people.

Project or creative space—this is open or enclosed space, designed, and dedicated specifically for project team working or brainstorming activities. Equipped with electronic whiteboards and other means of helping to assist the development of ideas and the capturing of knowledge.

Informal meeting area/social space/breakout space—a meeting space with a more informal feel to it. Often located in atriums or near main circulation or coffee points.

Crucial to making these changes has been an understanding of the potential impact of the workplace on the way an organization functions, and its interconnectedness with the information, communication, and technology (ICT) infrastructure, the human resource management framework and the organizational structure. Working Without Walls is the name the UK government has used to describe these many initiatives from a single perspective.

The experiences of a number of these trendsetting departments form the basis of this case study and their experiences outline the knowledge-enabling paybacks they have accrued through their various initiatives. These departments are Government Communications Headquarters (GCHQ), Her Majesty's Treasury (HMT), and the Ministry of Defense (MoD).

What Was the Outcome of the Response?

GCHQ: A new accommodations program was begun in 2000. Among the objectives of the program were creating a working environment to allow staff to interact more freely and effectively, and share knowledge more efficiently. Here are some of the statistical and anecdotal data that GCHQ has captured from the organization in response to the new accommodation changes:

- Increased interaction and visibility of staff has become quickly evident, with instances of staff seeing each other for the first time in years being reported. Opportunities for business-related conversations have increased dramatically and staff has to learn to become more focused and discriminatory in managing these encounters due to the additional time they can entail.
- The postoccupancy evaluation found that more than 80 percent of those surveyed were very pleased with the new layout, especially the breakout areas and meeting rooms, and believe the changes promote more interaction and communication.

HMT: Beginning in 1999, HMT begun to refurbish its building. Among the objectives of that refurbishment were to create a space to enable the Treasury to work collaboratively, openly, creatively, and innovatively. Here are some of the statistical and anecdotal data that HMT has captured from the organization in response to the refurbishment:

- HMT's postoccupancy evaluation of 2003 found that over 80 percent of employees surveyed believed the improved facilities increased interaction and all employees surveyed agreed that the new layout encourages collaboration and is improving communications and knowledge sharing.
- Since opening its redeveloped office HMT has experienced an unprecedented increase in the number of visitors to its building. Approximately 90 percent of visitors have been from other government bodies and have used both formal (such as conference rooms) and

informal spaces (such as the restaurant) to hold meetings and events. This degree of collaboration was not possible in HMT's previous environment.

MoD: redevelopment project of the MoD main building began in 2000. The previous accommodation was seen as a hindrance to the collaborative team working and knowledge sharing that the MoD wanted to encourage. In concert with the physical redevelopment, MoD has introduced an associated change management program (HOME; Head Office Modern Environment) for staff aimed at encompassing preparation for, and familiarization with, the new building and working practices, and subsequent measurement of the benefits it has achieved.

After the phased reoccupation of its main building through 2004, MoD decided that it wanted to install a robust benefits management approach to ensure it maximizes benefits from the changes it has introduced. It was believed that MoD needed to have a more in-depth capacity for assessing improvements in organizational capability and effectiveness. To address this requirement, MoD has implemented the following:

- A series of employee workshops was convened to categorize change program benefits, and to assess the ongoing management and measurement requirements of those benefits. Benefits were categorized into two types: enabling benefits, and business benefits. Enabling benefits (e.g., new environment, processes, and skills) are the foundations for the broader business changes to be built up and must be delivered first. Business benefits can be leveraged from the enabling benefits and are the responsibility of individual business units, who have developed change plans for maintaining the ownership and responsibility for delivering and measuring individual benefits.

- The following knowledge-focused benefit descriptors and targets were agreed upon:
- Environment: Improved knowledge sharing and creativity enabled through environmental design.
- Business unit exploitation of HOME: Improved knowledge sharing.
- Create flexible modern work environments: Improved efficiency, personal productivity, team working, and communication.
- Share facilities, resources, and information: Improved access to information and knowledge.

Take-Aways

Here are some of the lessons and value-added components that have emerged from the *Working Without Walls* initiative.

1. Recognize and exploit workplace change as an opportunity for business change.
2. Understand the business need and direct the workplace change toward delivering business benefits.
3. Make sure a plan is in place so that after the workplace change is complete the organization can take responsibility for realizing the long-term benefits of the business change.
4. Build an integrated project team to deliver an integrated long-term solution supported by senior management and with the appropriate accompanying development of HR policies, ICT connectivity, and staff management techniques in support of the new way of working.
5. Manage the change: Prepare people for the new workplace environment, communicate constantly about the change process, and actively seek and monitor user feedback.

6. Don't miss other opportunities for business change and improvement by focusing too narrowly on the accommodation need.

In Summary

The Working Without Walls case study is the most intriguing of all the ones I have included. Ostensibly not a KM initiative at all, and yet with profound implications for any organization planning to implement KM. The thought that environmental design can have a major impact on an organization planning to implement KM is worthy of anyone's consideration. Although there does not appear to be any longitudinal data available tracking what impact such an environment actually does have from a KM perspective, it would seem to make a lot of sense to believe that if you structure the workplace to facilitate meetings, then the likelihood is that improved organizational knowledge exchange will occur. Whatever the scope and intentions of your KM initiative, I believe there would be additional payback to the organization in including objectives of an environmental nature. These could be of as grand a scale as a complete organizational redevelopment program or as low-level as designating a dedicated work space where individuals and teams can meet and brainstorm. Either way, the need for a physical transformation of the workspace is now a consideration worthy of inclusion in any KM program or project.

CASE STUDY 5: NASA—WHERE ORGANIZATIONAL LEARNING IS LITERALLY A MATTER OF LIFE AND DEATH

The National Aeronautics and Space Administration (NASA) was formed by the US government in 1958 to replace the old research agency for aeronautics, the National Advisory Committee for Aeronautics (NACA). NASA is the government agency responsible for the United States' space program and long-term general aerospace research. A civilian organization, it conducts (or oversees) research into both civilian and military aerospace systems. Its vision is to improve life here, to extend life to there, and to find life beyond. Its mission is to understand and protect our home planet, to explore the universe and search for life, and to inspire the next generation of explorers.

What Was the Problem?

This story is about the evolution and deployment of a grass roots KM solution called the Process Based Mission Assurance Knowledge Management System or PBMA-KMS for short. The PBMA-KMS was developed by NASA's Office of Safety and Mission Assurance (OSMA) under the direction of Dr. Steve Newman. The OSMA realized that to support NASA's programs and projects better, it was necessary to provide a means of promoting greater collaboration and communication among NASA professionals in the safety, mission assurance, and risk management communities. This requirement was brought into even sharper focus by the tragic accident to the space shuttle Columbia in February of 2003, and the subsequent findings of the inquiry investigating the disaster.

What Was the Response to the Problem?

Stage 1: Steer for the Curve Ahead (1999–2001)

In 1999, the OSMA conducted a number of focus groups involving senior NASA experts in safety and mission assurance and program management, with the aim of providing a solid analytical platform to use in the design and development of their KM solution. Early design ideas were based in part on the GWU's KM Program, in particular the framework of the "Four Pillars of Knowledge Management" developed by the team at GWU. Using the input from their work groups and the GWU framework as a starting point, the OSMA began the development of a pioneering knowledge management system that would integrate KM theory with intuitive program management workflow knowledge architecture and the latest available information technologies.

Under pinning the evolution of the PBMA-KMS has been the knowledge architecture (KA) that NASA adopted as a result of the OSMA's initial problem analysis. It was decided early on that what was needed was a way to provide a framework and context for the effective integration of safety, risk management and mission assurance processes into the typical understanding of what comprises a program or project life cycle. In other words, an architectural framework that mimics the way that program and project managers and systems engineers, actually work. The KA framework (see Figure 8.1) is a matrix containing 40 cells that incorporates basic Deming-type plan/do/check elements. All work belongs under one of two potential stages of evolution: formulation or implementation. All content is divided into one of five potential categories: *policies*, which are described as rules and guidelines we need to follow; *planning*, which is described as defining and organizing the things we need to do; *processes*, which are described as doing the things we need to do; *program control*, which is described as checks and balances; and *verification and testing*. All activity is divided into one of eight potential categories: program management, concept development, acquisition, hardware design, software design, manufacturing, preoperational integration and testing, and, operations.

	Formulation			Implementation				
	1.0 Program Management	2.0 Concept Development	3.0 Acquisition	4.0 Hardware Design	5.0 Software Design	6.0 Manufacturing	7.0 Pre-Ops Int & Test	8.0 Operations
1. Policies *Rules and Guidelines We Need To Follow*	1.1	2.1	3.1	4.1	5.1	6.1	7.1	8.1
2. Planning *Defining and Organizing the Things We Need To Do*	1.2	2.2	3.2	4.2	5.2	6.2	7.2	8.2
3. Processes *Doing the Things We Need To Do*	1.3	2.3	3.3	4.3	5.3	6.3	7.3	8.3
4. Program Control *Checks and Balances*	1.4	2.4	3.4	4.4	5.4	6.4		8.4
5. Verification and Testing	1.5			4.5	5.5	6.5		

FIGURE 8.1   *Process based mission assurance knowledge architecture framework.*

The PBMA-KMS used a core set of KM functionalities that have the potential to serve all users. These include document repository; advanced search and retrieval functions; secure communities of practice or interest, and workgroups in general; a secure Web meeting environment; and a knowledge repository (expert finder). Particular attention was given to user accessibility as the PBMA-KMS was developed, and the Web site was designed and constructed to present a clear and uncluttered look, and to assist the user in the most effective and efficient way as they navigate the site.

All users of the PBMA-KMS have access to a number of different services. The OSMA categorizes these services under 11 generic content-types: links, benchmarking case studies, video nuggets, best practice document, lessons learned, compliance verification guidance material, communities of practice, standard security work groups, enhanced security work groups, Web-based secure meeting environment, and a knowledge repository.

A key milestone in the early stages of the PBMA-KMS was NASA's decision to allow it to be implemented through the functional organization (OSMA) responsible for its inception, rather than through a more traditional organizational lead such as the IT group or the chief information officer's (CIO) office. Thus the OSMA was able to address the organization's KM needs without having to wait for an information infrastructure to be put in place.

Stage 2: Run faster (2001–2004)

As a first stage in getting organizational buy in to the PBMA-KMS, a preview and workshop was held in connection with NASA's 2001 Assurance Technology Conference. During this workshop, one champion representing each of the NASA centers was trained in PBMA-KMS concepts and operation. These champions played a prominent role in the initial NASA center deployment activities that were completed between October 2001 and August 2002. Subsequent to these sessions, center champions have also been called on to assist in developing a functional discipline knowledge map for their center and identifying potential candidates for video nuggets, capturing tacit knowledge residing with center-based subject matter experts. Finally, the champions have been instrumental in the identification of potential work group managers for Communities of Practice based at their centers.

In 2001, the OSMA sponsored its first Community of Practice workshop. The workshop served to bring together work group managers to share information about starting, maintaining, and growing NASA working groups. In addition, presentations introducing the importance and implementation of KM were given to encourage the growth of the communities of practice across the agency. The workshop also provided several opportunities for the participants to be involved in group activities which developed various approaches to identifying knowledge in the agency and capturing and promoting it as a resource. The following year another workshop was held with the intention of bringing together work group managers to discuss various success stories and lessons learned for the existing communities of practice. In addition, presentations concerning IT security responsibilities and new or improved work group functionality were given. The workshop provided ample opportunity for attendees to participate in group activities to advance existing communities of practice to the next level and to help impact future direction for growth of knowledge management and communities of practice activities. The workshop is now an annual event, and subsequent meetings have served to stimulate the formation of communities within the new NASA Engineering and Safety Center and to bring together work group managers to discuss the dynamics and challenges of forming, operating, and maintaining a viable community of practice. In addition, the workshops have also showcased KM implementation experience from several leading US corporations as well as academic KM theory and practice and served as a medium to highlight IT security responsibilities and advertise new or improved work group functionality.

What Was the Outcome of the Response?

The PBMA-KMS is now available to all NASA personnel and serves NASA's program and project managers and safety and mission assurance professionals in a workflow context that mirrors their daily work processes. Over a 4-year period, the user community has grown to nearly 8000 members, with nearly 300 individual communities of practice in place and around 150 NASA programs and projects supported. The system is funded by the Agency Chief Safety and Mission Assurance Office and is therefore available at no cost to NASA employees, always an appealing value proposition to any prospective user.

In 2003, the PBMA-KMS received an eGov Pioneer award and in 2004 was recognized by NASA itself with its Civil Service/Contractor team award.

Available PBMA-KMS functions include the following:

Links: There are over 1500 links to NASA, the Department of Defense, Department of Energy (DOE), Department of Transportation (DOT), and the National Institute of Standards and Technology (NIST) policies and publications, aerospace industry standards and guidelines, lessons learned, and other PBMA-KMS resources such as workgroups and repositories, available.

Benchmarking case studies: Users have access to independent assessment reports for selected NASA programs and projects including NASA/Navy benchmarking exchange, shuttle superlightweight tank, orbital sciences, definition processes, shuttle ground operations, and the NASA expendable launch vehicle program.

Video nuggets: Users have access to over 300 video nuggets based on interviews with subject-matter experts from government, industry, and academia sharing insights on their experiences in various fields of safety, program/project management, engineering, and technology. Users have direct access to the full suite of Web-ready video interviews and can find specific video nuggets by a number of different search parameters. These nuggets not only provide enhanced interaction and utility for the users, but also supplement and complement other PBMA-KMS content.

Best practice documents: The best practices feature contains a vast library of documents from across NASA, representing virtually every one of its centers. Currently, the best practices library contains plans, process, and procedure documents; handbooks; manuals; requirements documents; analytical tools; test techniques; and more. The depth of documentation currently available offers immediate and wide-ranging utility for all PBMA-KMS users. Documents and links have been provided by NASA center directors in response to yearly call letters issued by the NASA associate administrator for safety and mission assurance.

Lessons learned: Provides users with links to NASA and other US government and worldwide aerospace lessons-learned Web sites. This functionality provides an important tool for planning successful missions. NASA and the entire aerospace industry continue to struggle to successfully incorporate lessons learned into their cultures. Issues of organizational instability, loss of corporate knowledge, reduction and elimination of historic standards and specifications, recruitment, and employee retention all pose formidable barriers to capturing lessons learned. Future expansion of lessons learned management capability in PBMA-KMS is planned, to assist in fostering greater utilization of lessons learned knowledge.

Compliance verification guidance material (CVG): CVG material was developed for selected NASA safety and mission assurance (SMA) policy directives and standards. The CVG material is presented in several formats intended to enhance user awareness and understanding of the SMA requirement and to help the user prepare for future SMA compliance verification audits. It is hoped that a heightened community awareness of SMA requirements will help foster the NASA safety culture, and lead to greater and more frequent access of official policy documents.

Communities of practice (CoP): The PBMA-KMS CoP has been a tremendous success. The NASA community is truly a global one in which partnerships and working relations exist between NASA researchers, program managers, assurance professionals, and their industry and international counterparts around the world. Building a community of knowledge is no longer confined to a single location, so individuals supporting assurance activities, particularly for an international project, can participate wherever they are. Available CoP tools include document exchange, bulletin boards, calendars, action-tracking, threaded discussion, subject-matter—expert clearinghouse, e-mail notification, general feedback, and collaboration.

Standard security work groups (SSWGs): Building on the foundation of the PBMA-KMS, an extensive user community participates in PBMA SSWG. The SSWG functionality has been very successful in fostering collaboration among the various NASA centers and other government, industry, and academic organizations. The SSWGs were initially started to help projects communicate more effectively but have now matured and changed with the needs of the users to support increasing communities (some with more than 400 users) and ever-increasing levels of security.

Enhanced security work groups (ESWGs): At the request of the user community, the PBMA team has deployed the only collaborative tools in NASA that are authorized to contain administratively controlled information such as competition sensitive, proprietary, and mishap investigation data. The ESWG functionality is a highly secure collaborative tool for NASA's programs and projects in need of working sensitive, but unclassified, projects from one centralized location.

SecureMeeting: SecureMeeting is a highly secure, behind-the-firewall Web conferencing solution for administratively controlled information data. SecureMeeting was designed to augment the agency-wide WebEx tool for those situations when the information being presented must not pass through a third party host. Functionality includes real-time collaboration in a secure environment, capable of holding 10 simultaneous meetings with 50 people in each; making changes in real-time; operating with standard Web browsers; and easy client setup, install, or download on-the-fly.

Knowledge registry: The Knowledge Registry is a continuously evolving product that works with NASA's competency management system (CMS) to inventory and locate safety, engineering, and technologic expertise throughout the agency and other government, industry, and academic organizations. Program and project managers can search the registry for individuals with real-world experience that can be applied to new programs and projects. The knowledge registry contains detailed information provided voluntarily by subject-matter experts.

By providing a broad range of knowledge management functional support to business users, the PBMA-KMS is playing a major role in NASA's attempt to transform its operations. For example, in support of the recommendations of the Columbia Accident Investigation Board, where there are currently 40 CoPs or work groups supporting the efforts of the space shuttle return-to-flight program.

In addition the PBMA-KMS was recently selected to host the NASA Administrator's Transformation Discussion Forum, which is a threaded discussion work space for NASA's senior leadership to gather employee ideas and promote discussion and dialog. The purpose is to actively engage the NASA community in transforming the agency's organizational structure and to address the recommendations of the Aldridge Commission and other external reports.

Stage 3: Keep on Running (2005—Ongoing)

Future directions and evolution for the PBMA-KMS includes the following:

- Increased user-interface functionality to address improved navigation, search, and retrieval capabilities (e.g., full-text search)
- Increased integration with other NASA safety and mission assurance applications
- Increased content access for public users
- Expansion of the knowledge registry module
- Meta-tagging for all data
- Repository storage for all content

Take-Aways

Here are some of the lessons and value-added components that have emerged from the development and deployment of the

PBMA–KMS:

1. Leadership

   a. Have a knowledge vision that ties to the corporate core competency.

   b. Sell the vision to a business unit leader who has their own budget.

   c. Involve management with implementation actions and demonstrate ROI through activity and results metrics.

   d. Recognize and use political toe-holds.

2. Organization

   a. Use an existing distributed organizational structure e.g., project managers, as an advocate network

   b. Forge partnerships with the IT, security, and training organizations.

3. Architecture

   a. Use natural structure (e.g., taxonomies) of rule—base organizations along with workflow to craft knowledge architecture.

   b. Avoid endless requirements analysis and let the work-flow define the information needs.

   c. Be mindful of security and legal (privacy, etc.) constraints.

   d. Focus on managing content from a business unit perspective.

4. Technology

   a. Use available organizational IT infrastructure where possible, but do not be afraid to create infrastructure where it is necessary to move beyond organizational inertia.

   b. Use COTS hardware and software whenever possible.

5. Communities and culture

   a. Establish champions in each business unit.

   b. Conduct annual workshops to bring together all champions.

   c. Develop communication tools such as posters and banners.

   d. Establish performance recognition and rewards.

Additionally, a special area of focus for NASA has been the Columbia accident investigation, and the many lessons learned from the investigation provide a useful case study of KM implementation in a crisis and emergency response situation. While NASA had contingency plans, policies, and procedures in place, one overarching lesson was that NASA also needed to have a Web-based investigation support system in place, specifically to support major mishaps. Furthermore, to keep pace with changes in the way organizations operate, KM support systems should develop an organization-wide hardware and software requirements baseline, and that baseline should be reviewed annually.

It was also seen to be essential to have a preselected and trained management team on standby to implement critical KM support activity in the event of a crisis.

Other lessons specific to support systems included the following:

- Have in place clear and fully documented IT security policies across all organizational centers for the care and management of sensitive information.
- Implement multiple Web-servers in parallel, to maximize system availability for critical Web-based applications. To the extent possible, duplicate a commercial

implementation configuration to ensure the greatest possible system reliability.

- Implement Web-based application software on a separate server from the file server. This approach allows routine large-file backup activity to take place on the file server without slowing down the Web server.
- Support storage, retrieval, and handling (opening and running) for a variety of large-file formats, including executable programs and hyperlinked PDF files from within the Web-based application.
- If it is deemed necessary to perform frequent and extensive file uploads, downloads, and manipulation, then it is important co-locate the Web servers with stand-alone archive/library servers because it is inefficient and time-consuming to transfer massive files via the Internet.
- Conduct traditional, multifunctional, end-to-end testing of all system components over the full range of operational scenarios, including different Internet routing and organizational firewall configurations.

In Summary

Finally, NASA's case study shows that no matter how well we think we are managing our knowledge, it is impossible to cover all the bases. NASA is an organization that has a superior level of knowledge in its workforce, as well as a mature and tested work environment that is focused on the exchange of knowledge and information. Yet, as the Columbia enquiry highlighted, there are still areas for improvement. When the managing of your knowledge is literally a matter of life and death to someone else, it definitely facilitates a *whatever it takes* kind of response to problem solving, and in NASA's case study that is exactly the approach the office (OSMA) responsible for the PBMA-KMS solution took. The OSMA steered a smart middle course in their drive to implement the PBMA-KMS, one that managed to move the project forward in a timely way without getting too bogged down in bureaucracy and red tape, and yet one that seems to have also kept everyone on board, even the IT group. The design of the PBMA-KMS tool was a true ground-up evolution, one that kept on evolving and incorporating best-of-the-best grass-roots technology and functionality, while still engaging the bureaucracy when and where necessary (e.g., in regards to IT security). This independence of purpose, while still maintaining an inclusive approach toward other groups in NASA, was what enabled the senior managers to feel comfortable enough to decide to delegate authority to the OSMA to develop and deploy the tool, instead of having the CIO organization do so as would have been normal practice.

TAKE-AWAY MENU

Here are five things worth remembering about implementing KM successfully:

1.   You cannot legislate for luck, either good or bad, in KM implementation, so plan for contingencies and be prepared to change plans and directions as needed.
2.   When looking to implement KM, avoid *build it and they will come* mindsets, as invariably *they* don't come.
3.   The creation of a core-design team, composed of individuals representing business areas from across the organization, will give any KM initiative a solid platform to start from.
4.   Whatever the KM vision that is driving KM implementation, try and ensure it links in some way to the organization's core competency.

5. Use available organizational IT infrastructure where possible, but do not be afraid to create infrastructure where it is necessary to move beyond organizational inertia or to facilitate community endorsement.

PART IV

THE DISAPPEARING PRESENT

NINE

Knowledge Management

The Next Generation

NOTHING ENDURES BUT CHANGE.

Heraclitus

I was watching a Robin Williams movie the other night called "The Final Cut," which got me thinking about what the future of knowledge management (KM) might look like. The premise of the movie was that at some future-time science will have advanced enough to have invented a virtual recording chip, one that gets implanted in us at birth and then records everything that happens to us throughout our lives. Once we die, the memory-bank chip is given to a *cutter* who has the responsibility of paring down a lifetime's recordings into a digestible 2-hour show that can be viewed posthumously by our loved ones and acquaintances. A tribute to our former glory that anyone and everyone can share in. Pretty much a metaphor for how KM works I thought. You take a lifetime of experience and turn it into a digestible sound-bite for someone else's benefit. A single conversation that can carry and covey a lifetime's experience, sometimes as part of something preplanned, and sometimes as the result of a chance encounter. In fact, I believe that the benefits of serendipitous knowledge are greatly underestimated and undervalued. After all, conversations are learning opportunities in the truest sense, and most of what we learn, and value, does not come through the orthodox routes of structured learning and organizational mandate, but rather through chance conversations and Web searches. So where does all that lead us in the move toward possible future evolutions of this thing we call knowledge management, and what technical advances will also help advance the cause of KM?

Today, most knowledge and information workers still rely on e-mail and voice mail for communication with individuals and teams. In fact a case could be made that the coming of e-mail heralded the advent of the knowledge age, and even knowledge management itself. The problem with e-mail is that, somewhat like Pandora's box, once it was opened it become an uncontrolled, and some would say uncontrollable, release mechanism for all that mankind knows, or at least wishes to share. In other words, a conduit for all of our communications desires. Interestingly enough, studies are showing that e-mail usage seems to follow cultural divides, with Europeans tending to use it in a more business-like fashion, whereas their North American counterparts are more likely to fill it with chatty and personalized information. Whatever our cultural background, we all struggle with the burden of information overload that e-mail has imposed on our daily lives. Yet it is truly a mechanism for sharing and collaborating with others, so it could be viewed as a KM-enabling tool, regardless of its potential ills. However, it is unlikely that the future evolution of KM will see any significant change in the status of e-mail as a KM enabler, and it will likely remain as a useful if somewhat problematic tool. One that at least helps with the desire to facilitate better sharing and collaborative business habits in the workplace.

Once e-mail arrived it was only a matter of time before technology caught up with the need that people have to be instantly in touch with the world wherever they are and whatever there working environment is. Hence the invention of instant messaging technology. Instant messaging is often now referred to as *IM*, much to the chagrin of information management practitioners who thought the use of the term IM was reserved for their own discipline. Many have heralded the arrival of instant messaging as a new opportunity for KM's evolution. Personally I do not quite see it that way. IM as a communication device enabling KM has no better credentials than did e-mail before it. It could well be used as a means of individual and team collaboration, but is far more likely to be used as a pared-down version of e-mail, one where fewer words are used to maintain the intent of fast communication, which is the whole basis of the appeal of instant messaging.

Finally, from a technical viewpoint there is the advent of Wikis, Blikis, CyborgLogs and WebLogs. CyborgLogs, or *Glogs* as they are often known, are the logs of technologic activities in which the person doing the recording was a participant. An example would be recordings made by assistive technologies such as a visual memory prosthetic, or a seeing aid that links to remote computational elements. In fact Glogs go back several decades to the birth of wearable computers in the 1970s, but modern technologies such as the camera-phone, has made the opportunity to create a Glog more available to everyday users. WebLogs, or Blogs as they are more often known as, have become fairly ubiquitous these days, and have even begun to take over the role of more traditional communication devices such as news outlets. They certainly can fulfill the role of being informative and knowledge-enabling, but they are also singular views and interpretations of what is happening in the world, and whether or not the information they contain is even truthful is very much down to the whims of the individual Blog owner. So neither Glogs nor Blogs could be described as being communal or collaborative in nature, and while they fulfill the purpose of sharing knowledge, they do not engage in knowledge exchange at all. Because of this lack of interaction in the Blogsphere, someone came up with the idea of the Bliki (also known as a WikiLog, WikiWeblog, Wikiblog, or Bloki). The Bliki is basically a Blog with interactive support in the way that a Wiki has. The combination of the two technologies is aimed at providing a more communal Blogging experience, one where information posted on the Blog can be edited by anyone or some group of authorized users. This is getting closer to a true KM-type of technology, and should help to improve the accuracy and quality of Blog postings, as well as help improve the fertilization of new ideas on Blogs.

The last and most KM-attuned new technology is the Wiki, named from the Hawaiian expression *wiki wiki* meaning quick or superfast. The Wiki is a Web site that allows users to add content, as on an Internet forum, but also allows anyone to edit the content. The term Wiki is also applied to the collaborative software used to create such a website. All in all, this is about the nearest any technology has come to the purest expression of the KM discipline, a completely open and transparent sharing and collaboration environment, accessible to all comers. It is generally accepted that the first Wiki, the Portland pattern repository, was created by Ward Cunningham in 1995, and since that date the concept of the Wiki has taken off. Particularly effective has been the creation of the Wikipedia, or electronic collaboration encyclopedia, in 2001. Based on the work of Jimbo Wales and Larry Sanger, who founded the Nupedia encyclopedia project, the Wikipedia is a marvel of sharing and collaborative endeavor. In fact when you use it you completely forget that the content was built piecemeal on a best-effort basis by numerous collaborators. I can definitely see this kind of collaborative technology being the way forward for organizations keen to capture their knowledge and experience in a virtual environment. Imagine the power of not just the present intellectual capital of the organization, but of those who have retired form the workforce, as well as communities of interest and other stakeholders, all combining to build a virtual repository of corporate knowledge. Why would this technology be more likely to succeed than the numerous commercial offerings already on the market that promise a collaborative workspace experience? Because I believe that Wikis come without all that historical and commercial baggage and are far more free-wheeling and less-restrictive in the way they operate, which is exactly the sort of environment that the new online generation can see itself working in. In other words, it fits nicely into a grassroots approach to providing KM solutions and that is where KM is at its most comfortable.

Apart from technology-based advances, what evolution are we likely to see in the way that KM works from a human perspective? Storytelling has recently been touted as the way forward for KM organizationally. Storytellers will obviously transfer significantly more context around experience and work practice than what is typically found in content form. You could even make the case that communities of practice or interest, are in fact excellent examples of the virtues of storytelling. However, few organizations that I have spoken to have expressed any interest whatsoever in storytelling as a focus of strategy, and it has always been the KM community itself who have seen it as a possible focus area. What that tells me is that storytelling is even further down the corporate-interest pecking order than KM itself. It is not that storytelling is not a powerful tool, it is. It is just that others have already staked out that particular part of the business landscape—lessons learned and best practices for example. Most organizational leaders do not have the time or inclination to indulge something that they see as being too lightweight and fluffy to be of direct or instant benefit to their desired business outcomes.

In the final analysis, the way that we as humans will interact with each other is unlikely to change very much, the real changes occur in the technology base that we utilize as our communications medium. A future where we all communicate by means of telepathy or other such mechanisms is as remote to us today as the basic technology of the telephone would have been to the cave man. We have advanced in an unparalleled fashion on the technology front over the last 100 years, and yet the basics of human expression, communication, and collaboration have barely changed in millennia. The only difference today is that technology has given us the power to reach millions, maybe even billions, when we communicate, whereas the last generation could only think of communicating with individuals or small groups of people at any one time. This instant connectivity has allowed for the evolution of knowledge communities and subject expertise from every conceivable perspective, many of them purely personal and noncommercial in nature. A good example of the way technology has provided a knowledge-sharing environment is the use of text messaging on cell phones. Text messaging provides individuals with a powerful means to communicate their thoughts and experiences to others and has become one of the main technology conduits that allows knowledge to flow around the globe in real time. Not KM in its true sense maybe, but nevertheless a vibrant knowledge sharing and reusing environment.

Finally, what is certain is that the human race has always been in the knowledge management business, and always will be. Organizations and senior managers may think that they are not doing KM, but the reality is that they are, whether they understand what it is or even want to acknowledge it as such. So, do not panic if things do not seem to be working out the way you had hoped and that there does not seem to be any corporate appetite for doing KM. Instead of worrying about the state of affairs, go into KM stealth mode instead if it helps and look to achieve knowledge-based changes in the way the organization operates in a subtler and less overt manner. By doing so you will be helping people to do what they have always done, manage their knowledge and collaborate with others to achieve their individual and collective goals and objectives.

TAKE-AWAY MENU

Here are five things worth remembering about the future state of KM:

1. The power of serendipitous knowledge gains is greatly underestimated, so facilitate those opportunities as often as is possible through the use of communal workspace design and interactive work habits.

2. Storytelling can be a powerful tool, so look to increase knowledge about KM and establish a corporate comfort zone for it through the dissemination of KM success stories to those individuals who are most likely to fuel the corporate grapevine.

3. Communication tools such as e-mail have made it easier to share and collaborate with others, but do not expect them to become the tools of choice for KM practitioners any time soon, as they also encourage volume above focused content and using them as KM tools tends to be too time consuming.

4. Blogs can be a powerful tool for sharing, if not collaborating on, knowledge, but by their very nature they work best as vehicles for individual expression. Trying to use

them as a potential tool for company communications purposes is not a good fit for the way they work best.

5. Wikis seem to be an ideal tool for furthering corporate KM goals and outcomes, as they are true sharing and collaborating environments that grow both individual as well as organizational knowledge and competency.

Bibliography

Allee, Verna. *The Knowledge Evolution.* Burlington, MA: Butterworth Heinemann, 1997.

Bennett, Alex and David. *Organizational Survival in the New World.* Burlington, MA: KMCI Press, 2004.

Boswell, James and R. W. Chapman (eds.). *Life of Johnson,* London: Oxford University Press, 1998.

Boyd, Christopher. "Developing Practical Metrics at Wilson Sonsini." *KM Review,* Jan.—Feb. 2004 (vol. 6, no. 6).

Conway, Susan and Sligar, Char. *Unlocking Knowledge Assets.* Microsoft Press, 2002.

Denning, Stephen. *The Springboard.* Burlington, MA: KMCI Press, 2001.

Duffy, Jan. *Reaping the Benefits of Knowledge.* ARMA International, 1999.

Frid, Randy. *Frid Framework for Enterprise Knowledge Management.* Adobe Reader eBooks, 2004. ISBN 0-595-30699-3, or see *www.frid.com.*

Horibe, Frances. *Managing Knowledge Workers.* Hoboken, NJ: John Wiley & Sons, 1999.

Humes, James C. and Nixon, Richard M. *The Wit & Wisdom of Winston Churchill.* New York: Harper Perennial, 1995.

Kaplan, Robert and Norton, David. *The Balanced Scorecard.* Boston: Harvard Business School Press, 1996.

Laertius, Diogenes. *Lives of Eminent Philosophers.* Boston: Harvard University Press (Loeb Classical Library), 1925.

Lau, Theodora. *Best Loved Chinese Proverbs*. New York: Harper Perennial (1st ed.), 1995.

Lieberman, Gerald. *3,500 Good Quotes for Speakers*. St. Charles, MO: Main Street Books, 1987.

Liebowitz, Jay. *Knowledge Management Handbook*. CRC Press, 1999.

Marcus, Robert and Watters, Beverley. *Collective Knowledge*. Microsoft Press, 2002.

McKeen, James and Smith, Heather. *Marketing KM to the Organization*. Ontario, Canada: Queen's University, KM Forum (vol. 5, no. 2), 2003. (See *business.queensu.ca/knowledge/workingpapers/working/working_04-20.pdf*)

Mencken, H. L. *Definitions, Skepticisms, Irreverences, Observations, Barbs and Other Acerbities: A Collection of Quotations from H.L. Mencken*. San Francisco: Arion Press, 1995.

Pfeiffer, William. *RoadKill on the Information Highway*. San Francisco: Pfeiffer & Company, 1999.

Pritchett, Price. *New Work Habits For A Radically Changing World*. Dallas, TX: Pritchett & Associates, Inc. 1994.

Richard, Elisabeth. *Archetypes of the Network Age: Articulating the New Public Service Reality*. PWGSC Publications, Public Works and Government Services Canada (Public Policy Forum), 2003. ISBN 0-9732003-7-5.

Rossiter, John R. and Percy, Larry. *Advertising Communications and Promotion Management*. New York: McGraw-Hill Companies (2nd ed.), 1997.

Smith, Heather and McKeen, James. Valuing the Knowledge Management Function, *Handbook on KM*, Vol. 2. New York: Springer, 2003.

Sowell, Thomas. *Knowledge and Decisions*. New York: Basic Books (reprint ed.), 1996.

Stewart, Thomas. *The Wealth of Knowledge*. Nicholas Brealey, 2001.

Sveiby, Karl Erik. *The New Organizational Wealth*. San Francisco: Berret-Koehler Inc., 1997.

Tapscot, Don; Lowy, Alex and Ticoll, David. *Blueprint for the Digital Economy*. New York: McGraw-Hill, 1998.

Wenger, Etienne; McDermott, Richard and Snyder, William. *Cultivating Communities of Practice*. Boston: Harvard Business School Press, 2002.

Wilde, Oscar. *The Plays of Oscar Wilde: Lady Windermere's Fan and a Woman of No Importance* (Wordsworth Collection, Vol. 1). New York: NTC/Contemporary Publishing Company (McGraw-Hill), 1998.

Zack, Michael. "Developing a Knowledge Strategy." Berkeley, CA: *California Management Review* 41/3 (Spring 1999), p. 125–146.

INDEX

Page numbers followed by "f" denote figures; page numbers followed by "t" denote tables.

A

Accessibility, of knowledge, as KM principle, 63, 78

Accountability, as KM principle, 63, 77

Acquisition, in NASA KM program, 175, 176f

Action plan, for aligning KM, 54, 56

Activity measures, in KM assessment, 34

Agency Chief Safety and Mission Assurance Office, of NASA, 179

Airlines, using FAA KM, 140

Aldridge Commission, 183

Aligning knowledge management, 47–68

action plans for, 54, 56

business goals and, 54

central group importance in, 85–86

competency identification in, 65–66

corporate capacity and, 62–65

current situation analysis in, 53

demonstrable outcomes in, 66–67

dependencies in, 56–57

different organizational requirements and, 67–68

guiding principles for, 58–60

implementation in, 60–66

obstacles to, 48

personalized approaches to, 58

pilot projects in, 59–60, 67

priorities in, 59–60

promotion in, 55, 64–65

quick wins in, 60–61

risks in, 56–58

Aligning knowledge management
(*continued*)
stakeholder identification in,
55–56, 65
starting point for, 52–53
strategies for. *see* Strategies, for
aligning KM
America On Line (AOL), as
example for FAA KM
program, 141
American Productivity and Quality
Center, KMAT assessment
tool of, 34
Anecdotal measures, of KM, 97
AOL (America On Line), as
example for FAA KM
program, 141
Arthur Anderson, KM assessment
tool of, 33–34
Assessment, of KM. *see also*
Measuring knowledge
management
for alignment, 53
for deployment, 78–79
for marketing, 34–36, 35t, 37f,
38
Asset management, deploying KM
and, 79
Associate Administrators group, of
FAA KM, 140
Assurance Technology Conference,
in NASA KM program,
177–178
Audience, for marketing, 27–28,
39–40, 42, 44
Audits
information asset register tool kit
for, 151
for measuring KM, 99–103
Australian Bureau of Statistics,
157–166
description of, 157–158

knowledge strategy of
behavior development for, 161
infrastructure of, 158–161
outcome of, 161–164
Awareness, of KM, 29–30, 63–64
Awareness sessions, for marketing,
29

B
Baby-boomer generation
employee attrition in, 57–58
impact of, on government, 14
Balanced scorecard, for measuring
KM, 101–103
Basic needs, for marketing, 32, 37f,
39–41
Behavior measures, in KM
assessment, 34
Benchmarking case studies, in
NASA KM program, 177,
179–180
Best practice documents, in NASA
KM program, 177, 180
Birmingham City Council,
Comprehensive
Performance Assessment
improving and planning
for, 151–153
Blikis, 193–194
Blogs (WebLogs), 154–155,
193–194
Blokis (Blikis), 193–194
Bottom-up approach, to deploying
KM, 73
Boyd, Christopher, in KM metrics,
92
Brainstorming, creative spaces for,
169
Brand attitude, 27, 29–30
Brand awareness, 29–30
Brand purchase intention, 27
Brochure, on KM, 64

Business(es)
    incompetence in, 7–8
    indifference to KM, 17
Business leaders, as target
        audience, 44
Business managers, marketing to,
        28
Business model, KM strategy based
        on, 48–49, 49f
Business plans, in aligning KM, 52
Business process analysis, 43
Business process owners, in
        aligning KM, 56
Business processes
    management of, in Australian
        Bureau of Statistics,
        164–165
    measuring KM and, 94f
    re-engineering of, information
        asset register tool kit for, 151
Business strategies
    evaluation of, in measuring KM,
        108t
    KM strategy aligned with, 50–52,
        115–117
    support of, 117

C
Camden, London Borough of, KM
        roadmap for, 148–150
Camera phone, 193
Canada, Public Works and
        Government Services
        Canada. see Public Works
        and Government Services
        Canada
Canadian Institute of Knowledge
        Management
    assessment tool of, 34
    Knowledge Management
        Maturity Survey of, 101–102
    roadmap of, 70–72, 71f

Capacity check or audit, for
        measuring KM, 99–103
Capital, human, purpose of, 16
Case studies
    Australian Bureau of Statistics,
        157–166
    Federal Aviation Administration
        knowledge services network,
        135–143
    Knowledge Management
        National Project (United
        Kingdom), 143–157
    NASA KM program, 177,
        179–180
    National Aeronautics and Space
        Administration, 173–187
    Working Without Walls initiative
        (United Kingdom),
        166–173
Cell phones, text messaging on, 196
Central information technology
        group, of FAA, 139
Central knowledge management
        group, 33–36, 35t, 37f,
        85–86, 118
Change
    in culture, 86
    on daily basis, 4
    in governments, resistance
        to, 3–5
    in large institutions, 5
    management of, 84–85
    in personnel, 72–73
    program for, in Working
        Without Walls initiative,
        171–172
    for success in information age, 15
    Trojan Horse concept in, 17
China, Team Canada mission to, 4
Churchill, Winston
    on change, 91
    on success, 133

Client service teams
  KM techniques for, 82
  marketing to, 28
Climate, organizational, evaluation
    of, in measuring KM, 98t
Cluster managers, marketing to, 24
Collaborative approaches
  in Australian Bureau of Statistics,
    159, 162
  to deploying KM, 77, 80–81, 87,
    136–137
  to marketing, 45
  in NASA, 174, 182
  software for, 80–81, 136
Columbia space shuttle accident,
    174
  investigation board for, 183
  lessons learned from, 185
Common services integrators,
    marketing to, 24
Communication
  about successful KM, 29–30
  Blogs in, 154–155, 193–194
  clear language in, 86
  constant, 86–87
  in deploying KM, 85–87
  e-mail in, 192–193
  evaluation of, in measuring KM,
    98t
  instant messaging in, 127, 193
  of KM benefits, 123–124
  of KM measurement results, 122
  as KM principle, 63, 64
  lack of, KM failure in, 85
  in local government roadmap,
    150
  objectives of, 64
  officials working in, marketing
    to, 24
  targeted, 87
  by telepathy, 196
  voice mail in, 192

in Working Without Walls
    initiative, 169
Communities
  evaluation of, in measuring KM,
    109t
  in FAA KM program, 142–143
  knowledge management in, 14
  support for, in local government
    roadmap, 150
Communities of practice
  marketing to, 28
  in NASA KM program, 177, 178,
    181, 185
Community Knowledge in Policy
    Development Project,
    156–157
Competency
  evaluation of, in measuring KM,
    109t
  promotion of, 65–66
Competency management system,
    in NASA KM program, 182
Compliance verification guidelines,
    in NASA KM program,
    177, 181
Comprehensive Performance
    Assessments, for UK city
    councils, 151–153
Concept development, in NASA
    KM program, 175, 176f
Connectivity, in virtual world, 4
Consultation, for deploying KM,
    87
Consultation staff, marketing to, 24
Content management, 43
Contextualizing, of knowledge, 83
Continuity, of personnel, 72–73
Conway, Susan, on
    communication, 85
Cookbooks, for service delivery, by
    local governments, 151–153

Coordination, for deploying
    DM, 77
Corporate resources, KM
    competing with, 25
Creative space, in Working Without
    Walls initiative, 169
Crisis situations, KM support in,
    185–186
Culture
    knowledge, in measuring KM,
        102
    of NASA KM program, 185
    organizational
        change in, 86
        evaluation of, in measuring
            KM, 98t
Cunningham, Ward, Wiki
    development by, 194
Customer(s)
    focus on, in local government
        roadmap, 149–150
    KM focus on, 58–59
    measuring KM and, 94f,
        102, 122
    response time for, 122
    teams responsible for
        KM techniques for, 82
    marketing to, 28
Customer relationship
    management, 32, 82
Customer-Facing Program, for
    local governments, 153
Customization, of KM
    measurement, 122
Customized matrix, for measuring
    KM, 103–105
CyborgLogs (Glogs), 193–194

D
Data, disorganized, 36
Databases

administration of, as basic
    need, 32
work group, in Australian Bureau
    of Statistics, 162–165
Decision making, facilitation of,
    75–76
    KM measurement and, 121
    local intelligence systems for,
        150–151
    at strategic needs level, 44
Demographics, impact of, on
    government, 14
Dependencies, evaluation of, in
    aligning KM, 56–57
Deploying knowledge management,
    69–90
    actions for, 70–72, 71f
    bottom-up approach to, 73
    change fatigue in, 72–73
    checklist for, 71–72
    at FAA, 135–143
    grassroots approach to, 73
    guiding principle set for, 76–78
    obstacles to, 69–72
    potential outcomes of, 87–89
    questions in, 73–76
    realistic expectations for, 84–87
    roadmap for, 70–72, 71f
    strategies for, 78–80
    supporting tools and processes
        for, 80–84
    template for, 82–84
    top-down approach to, 73
Document repository, in NASA
    KM program, 177

E
Education
    for aligning KM, 65–66
    in Australian Bureau of
        Statistics, 161
    for deploying KM, 75, 87, 161

Education (*continued*)
for knowledge workers, 80–81
as metric for KM, 106
in NASA KM program, 177–179
eGov Pioneer award, for NASA KM
program, 179
E-mail
in Australian Bureau of Statistics,
162–163
in deploying KM, 80, 127–128
Employees
accountability of, 77
education of, 54, 65–66, 75
evaluation of, in measuring
KM, 104
expectations of, for KM, 74–75
involvement in KM, as
metric, 106
KM competency in, 65–66
KM irrelevance to, 18
knowledge transfer from, 66
location of, in Working Without
Walls initiative, 168
satisfaction of, with Working
Without Walls initiative, 167
Employment, rules of, 8
Enabling needs, for marketing,
32–33, 37f, 41–43
Encyclopedias, electronic, 194
Engineering and Safety Center,
NASA, 178–179
Enhanced security work groups, in
NASA KM program,
177, 182
Enterprise document systems, 79
European Union, Directive on
Re-use of Public Sector
Information, 151
Evaluation, of KM. *see* Measuring
knowledge management
Evidential measures, of KM, 97

Experiences, with KM. *see* Lessons
learned
Explicit knowledge strategy, of
Australian Bureau of
Statistics, 160

F
Federal Aviation Administration
(FAA), knowledge services
network of, 135–143
Financial perspective, in measuring
KM, 94f, 104
Focus groups
for deploying KM, 76, 174–175
for measuring KM, 94
Ford, Henry, on history, 133
Four pillars model, for KM
framework, 137, 175
Freedom of Information Act,
compliance with,
information asset register
tool kit for, 151
Frid, Randy, on market spin, 40
Front-line officers, marketing
to, 24
Future capabilities, evaluation of,
in measuring KM, 98t

G
General Manager, of FAA KM
program, 141
Geographical information system
technology, for rural
intelligence, 156
George Washington University,
four pillars model of,
137, 175
Global village, 4
Glogs (CyborgLogs), 193–194

Government(s)
    electronic technology for, 5, 6
    fragmentation in, 9–10
    hoarding knowledge by, 15
    incompetence in, 7–8
    intellectual capital of, 16
    job security in, 8
    Knowledge Management
        National Project (United
        Kingdom), 6–7, 9, 143–157
    knowledge organization in, 5
    public expectations of, 4
    rapid management changes in, 7
    resistance to change, 3–5
    as single organizational entity, 9
    strict policies of, 14
Government Communications
        Headquarters department
        (United Kingdom),
        workplace modifications in,
        169–170
Government responsible
        individual, in FAA KM
        program, 142
Government Telecommunications
        and Informatics Service, 24
Grassroots approach, to deploying
        KM, 73

H
Happiness, measurement of, 97
Hardware design, in NASA KM
        program, 175, 176f
Head Office Modern Environment,
        in Working Without Walls
        initiative, 171
Heraclitus, on change, 191
Her Majesty's Treasury, workplace
        modifications in, 170–171
History, of KM. see Lessons learned
Horizontality of knowledge, 5,
        63, 78

Human capital, purpose of, 16
Human resources
    for deploying KM, 79–80
    KM interdependency with,
        57, 102

I
IBM Lotus eMail, for KM, 128
IM (instant messaging), 127, 193
Improvement and Development
        Agency, Knowledge
        Management National
        Project and, 144
Informal spaces, in Working
        Without Walls initiative, 169
Information asset register tool
        kit, 151
Information Communications
        Technology, for local
        governments, 152
Information management
    as basic need, 32
    Canadian legislation on, 69–70
    for deploying KM, 79
    vs. information technology,
        47, 125
    vs. KM, 124–126
    KM competing with, 25
    KM supporting, 125–126
    transition of, to KM, 148–150
    in Working Without Walls
        initiative, 169
Information processes, disjointed
        and disconnected, 36
Information synthesists, marketing
        to, 24
Information technology
    anarchy in, 81
    central group of, in FAA, 139
    for deploying KM, 77–79
    vs. information management,
        47, 125

Information technology (*continued*)
    KM added value to, 40–41
    KM competing with, 25
    KM interdependency with, 57
    KM supporting, 125–126
    in KM usage, 126–128
    in Working Without Walls
        initiative, 169
Infrastructure
    for Australian Bureau of Statistics
        KM, 158–161, 163–164
    for deploying KM, 77–79
    designed for knowledge
        sharing, 63
    improvement of, 88–89
    interconnectedness of, in
        Working Without Walls
        initiative, 169
Instant messaging, 127, 193
Intellectual capital, value of, 48
Intelligence systems, local, 150–151
Intranet, 84, 106, 122
Introduction to the Desktop course, of
        Australian Bureau of
        Statistics, 161

J
Jargon, avoidance of, 86
Job security, 8
Johnson, Samuel, on knowledge, 47

K
Kaplan, Robert, on balanced
        scorecard, 92, 103
KM. *see* Knowledge management
KMAT (Knowledge Management
        Assessment Tool), 34
KMS2000 technology, 137
Knowing organization, 48
Knowledge
    accumulated, 35
    analysis of, in deploying KM, 83

    availability of, in measuring
        KM, 106
    capturing
      explicit, 57
      tacit, 57, 154–155
    context of, in deploying KM, 83
    current use of, in measuring
        KM, 104
    exchange of, for deploying
        DM, 77
    flow patterns of, 81
    future use of, in measuring
        KM, 107
    horizontality of, 5
    individual, development and
        application of, 81–82
    measuring KM and, 94f
    retention of, measurement
        of, 102
    reuse of, 102
    sharing of. *see* Communication;
        Sharing knowledge
    as strategic asset, 48, 77
    tools for, in measuring KM, 102
Knowledge architecture, in NASA
        KM program, 175, 176f, 184
Knowledge assets, 35
Knowledge capital, exploiting, 57
Knowledge charter, 64
Knowledge competence,
        improvement of, 89
Knowledge day, 65
Knowledge dependency, 35
Knowledge directory
    for deploying KM, 79–80
    for marketing, 32, 35
    as metric, 106
Knowledge domains, 35
Knowledge intensity, improvement
        of, 88

Knowledge management
  assessment of, 34–36, 35t, 37f,
    38. *see also* Measuring
    knowledge management
  for alignment, 53
  for deployment, 78–79
  business sponsor for, 62
  case for, 55
  central office for, 33–36,
    35t, 37f
  corporate leader for, 29
  corporate policy for, 62
  definition of, 5, 16–17, 55,
    128–130
    for KM National Project, 146
    variation in, 118–119
  development of, from
    information management,
    148–150
  environment favorable for, 14–15
  evaluation of. *see* Measuring
    knowledge management
  experiences with. *see* Lessons
    learned
  failure of, 29, 123–124
  future of, 191–198
  guiding principles for, 58–60
  history of, 47–48
  improvements due to, 88–89
  vs. information management,
    124–126
  irrelevance of, 18
  marketing of. *see* Marketing
  maturity of, assessment of,
    34–36, 35t, 37f, 38,
    78–79, 100–103, 120
  name selection for, 30–31
  need for, 15
  objectives of, 50, 54, 86, 116
  as old concept, 14
  perception of, 118–119
  purpose of, 48

relevance of, 18–19, 74
  success stories about, 29–30, 67
  supporting role of, 17–18,
    125–126
  value of, 13–14
Knowledge Management
    Assessment Tool
    (KMAT), 34
Knowledge Management
    Community Knowledge in
    Policy Development
    Project, 156–157
Knowledge Management Maturity
    Survey, 100–103
Knowledge Management National
    Project (United Kingdom),
    6–7, 9, 143–157
  aims of, 144
  community knowledge in policy
    development for Leeds and
    Newcastle, 156–157
  Comprehensive Performance
    Assessment improvement
    for Birmingham City
    Council, 151–153
  customer-facing program for
    London Borough of Tower
    Hamlets, 153
  KM roadmap for London
    Borough of Camden,
    148–150
  local intelligence systems and
    information asset registers
    for Wilshire County,
    150–151
  problem facing, 144–146
  response to problem, 146–148
  rural intelligence tool kit for
    Wiltshire County, 155–156
  tacit knowledge capture for
    London Borough of
    Lewisham, 154–155

Knowledge Management
    Strengthening
    Communities in Rural
    Areas project, 155–156
Knowledge Management Value
    Assessment tool, 34
Knowledge mapping
  as basic need, 32
  as metric, 106
Knowledge mobilization, 30, 129
Knowledge navigation aids, as basic
    need, 32
Knowledge organizations,
    148–149
Knowledge practices, evaluation
    of, 52
Knowledge processes, in measuring
    KM, 100
Knowledge registry, in NASA KM
    program, 182
Knowledge repository, in NASA
    KM program, 177
Knowledge responsibility, 35
Knowledge services network,
    135–143
Knowledge visibility, improvement
    of, 88
Knowledge workers
  in aligning KM, 55–56
  as marketing target, 38–39
  support for, 80–84

L
Leadership
  in aligning KM, 49f
  evaluation of, in measuring KM,
    97t
  for KM program, 184
Learning
  in aligning KM, 49f
  barriers to, 5

organizational, in local
    government roadmap, 150
Learning organization, 48
Leeds City Council, Community
    Knowledge in Policy
    Development project of,
    156–157
Legislation, as obstacle for KM,
    69–70
Lessons learned, 113–131
  business strategy importance,
    115–117
  caveats with, 114–115
  different definitions of KM,
    118–119
  information management vs.
    knowledge management,
    124–126
  measurement importance,
    120–123
  NASA KM program, 177,
    179–180, 184–186
  perception importance, 123–124
  position of surveys, 119–120
  problems with, 114
  technology importance,
    126–128
  terminology for KM, 128–130
  value of, 114–115
Lewisham, London Borough, tacit
    knowledge capture program
    for, 154–155
Links, in NASA KM program,
    177, 179
Local Authority Web sites National
    Project, 153
Local intelligence systems, 150–151,
    155–156
Local Strategic Partnerships, in
    local government, 156–157
Lotus eMail, for KM, 128

Low-hanging fruit, in aligning KM,
　60–61
Luck, in KM programs, 134

M
McKeen, Jim, on KM assessment,
　35t, 37f
Managers. *see also* Senior managers
　in aligning KM, 55–56, 66–67
　knowledge charter for, 64
　marketing to, 24, 28
　in measuring KM, 107–109
　skepticism in, 69
　workshops for, in NASA KM
　　program, 178
Manufacturing, in NASA KM
　　program, 175, 176f
Marketing, 23–46
　assessment for, 34–36, 35t, 37f
　for basic needs, 32, 36, 37f,
　　38–41
　brand attitude in, 27, 29–30
　challenges to, 24–25, 27–30, 41,
　　43, 45
　for enabling needs, 32–33, 37f,
　　41–43
　engagement strategies for, 28,
　　40, 42, 44
　expectation level in, 23–24
　to governments, 9
　name selection for, 128–130
　need identification in, 26–29,
　　32–36, 35t, 37f
　objectives of, 26, 39, 41–42, 44
　overview of, 37f
　plan for, 31–36
　of Process Based Mission
　　Assurance Knowledge
　　Management System
　　(NASA), 177–179
　reasons for, 25–27
　skills for, 25–26, 41, 43, 45

spin for, 37f, 40, 42, 44
　for strategic needs, 33–36, 35t,
　　37f, 44–45
　target audience for, 27–28,
　　39–40, 42, 44
Maslow's Hierarchy of Needs,
　for marketing, 26
Matrix, customized, for measuring
　KM, 103–105
Mean time to repair, as
　measurement, 122
Measuring knowledge management,
　91–109
　at business-unit level, 121–122
　in FAA program, 140–141
　lack of generic metrics for,
　　92–93
　mechanisms for, 99–109
　　balanced scorecard, 103–105
　　capacity check or audit, 99–103
　　customized matrix, 105–107
　　selection of, 120–123
　　strategic framework, 107–109
　metric selection for, 96
　organizational perspectives of,
　　93–94, 94f
　quantitative vs. qualitative, 96–97
　questions needed for, 95
　reasons for, 91–96, 94f
　stealth in, 121
　surveys in, 100–103, 119–120
Meeting spaces, in Working
　　Without Walls initiative, 169
Mencken, H. L., on government, 3
Mentorship programs, 66
Meta-data
　in Australian Bureau of Statistics,
　　162–163
　in Tacit Knowledge Project,
　　154–155
Metrics. *see* Measuring knowledge
　　management

Microsoft
  KM assessment tool of, 34
  Outlook, for KM, 128
Ministry of Defense (United
  Kingdom), workplace
  modifications in, 171–172
Motivation, evaluation of, in
  measuring KM, 97t

N
NASA. *see* National Aeronautics and
  Space Administration;
  Process Based Mission
  Assurance Knowledge
  Management System
National Aeronautics and Space
  Administration
  description of, 173–174
  Engineering and Safety Center
  of, 178–179
  KM program of. *see* Process
  Based Mission Assurance
  Knowledge Management
  System
  using FAA KM, 140
National Airspace System, of FAA
  KM, 140
Needs
  assessment of, 34–36, 35t
  basic, 32, 37f, 39–41
  constant changes in, 28
  creation of, 29–30
  definition of, 26
  enabling, 32–33, 37f, 41–43
  identification of, 26, 28–29
  product selection for, 26–27
  strategic, 33–37, 35t, 37f, 44–45
Newcastle City Council,
  Community Knowledge
  in Policy Development
  project of, 156–157

Newman, Steve, NASA program
  developed by, 174
Nodes/node administrators/node
  facilitators, in FAA KM
  program, 141–142
Norton, David, on balanced
  scorecard, 92, 101
Nupedia encyclopedia project, 194

O
Object management strategy, of
  Australian Bureau of
  Statistics, 160–163
Office of Safety and Mission
  Assurance, NASA, 174–178
Operations, in NASA KM
  program, 175, 176f
Operations Center, of FAA KM,
  140
Organization
  in aligning KM, 49f
  of KM program, 184
  of knowledge, 5
Orientation sessions, for KM, 75
Outcomes, consideration of
  in deployment, 75–76, 84–89
  in marketing, 28
Outlook, Microsoft, for KM, 128
Outreach sessions, for marketing,
  29

P
Path of least resistance, in KM
  introduction, 18
Payback, for deploying KM, 75–76
People
  in aligning KM, 49f, 54–56, 58
  metrics focused on, 97
Percy, Larry, on needs, 26
Performance evaluation,
  in measuring KM,
  34, 103, 97t

Personal holdings e-mail application, of Australian Bureau of Statistics, 162–163
Personnel records, in KM assessment, 34
Pilot projects
  in aligning KM, 59–60, 67
  in implementing KM, 137–138
Plan
  in aligning KM, 54, 56
  marketing, 31–36
    for basic needs, 32
    for enabling needs, 32–33, 37f
    KM name in, 129–130
    for strategic needs, 33–36, 35t, 37f
Planning
  in FAA KM program, 142
  as KM principle, 63, 77
  in NASA KM program, 175, 176f
  organizational, measuring KM and, 101
Policy development
  in NASA KM program, 175, 176f
  tool kit for, 156–157
Policy officials, marketing to, 24
Portland pattern repository, 194
Preoperational integration and testing, in NASA KM program, 175, 176f
Pritchett, Price, on change in work habits, 15
Process(es)
  in aligning KM, 54, 58
  in measuring KM, 104
  in NASA KM program, 175, 176f
Process Based Mission Assurance Knowledge Management System (NASA), 174–188
  core functionalities of, 177
  development of, 174–177, 176f

future directions and evolution of, 183
  knowledge architecture in, 175, 176f
  lessons learned from, 177, 179–180, 184–186
  marketing of, 177–179
  present functions of, 179–183
  workshops on, 177–179
Process control portals, in Australian Bureau of Statistics KM, 164
Process improvement, criteria for, 71–72
Process knowledge management, in Australian Bureau of Statistics, 164–165
Process redesign, in deploying KM, 82
Process selection, in deploying KM, 82
Productivity
  in Australian Bureau of Statistics operation, 162
  KM support of, 51
Program control, in NASA KM program, 175, 176f
Program management, in NASA KM program, 175, 176f
Program officers, marketing to, 24
Project managers and project management
  aligning KM and, 61
  deploying KM and, 79
  marketing to, 28
Project space, in Working Without Walls initiative, 169
Promotional activities
  for aligning KM, 55, 64–65
  for marketing, 29
Propaganda, for KM program, 123–124

Public Policy Forum, Canada, 24
Public Works and Government
    Services Canada
    assessment tool of, 34
    deploying KM in, 71–72, 126
    KM definition of, 16–17, 118–119
    KM name selection in, 31
    managerial turnover in, 7
    measuring KM in, 100–103, 120
Publicity, for KM program,
    123–124

Q
Qualitative measures, of KM,
    96–97
Quality assurance, as KM principle,
    63, 78
Quantitative measures, of KM,
    96–97
Quick wins, in aligning KM, 60–61

R
Records management, 79, 124–125
    in Australian Bureau of Statistics,
        160–161
Research projects, information
    asset register tool kit for, 151
Return on investment
    in aligning KM, 54
    in marketing, 24–25
    in measuring KM, 93
Risks, evaluation of, in aligning
    KM, 56–58
Roadmap
    for deploying KM, 70–72, 71f
    for London Borough of
        Camden, 148–150
Rural intelligence tool kit, for
    Wiltshire County, 155–156

S
Safety and mission assurance policy,
    in NASA KM program,
    177, 181
Sales analysis, KM techniques for,
    82
Sanger, Larry, as Nupedia founder,
    194
Sarbanes-Oxley legislation, 70
Scorecard, balanced, for measuring
    KM, 103–105
Search and retrieval functions, in
    NASA KM program, 177
Secure meeting environments, in
    NASA KM program,
    177, 182
Selling. see Marketing
Senior managers
    in aligning KM, 55–56, 66–67
    in deploying KM, 86
    on knowledge as asset, 116
    in measuring KM, 107–109
    as target audience, 44
Serendipitous knowledge, 192
Services delivery, by local
    governments
    cookbooks for, 151–153
    customer-facing programs for,
        153
    Tacit Knowledge Project for,
        154–155
Sharing knowledge
    in Australian Bureau of Statistics,
        161–164
    disadvantages of, 85
    infrastructure for, 63
    measurement of, 102
    support for, 85–87
    trust for, 15–16
    in Working Without Walls
        initiative, 170

Siemens, knowledge management in, 9, 114–115

Simmons, Ron, FAA KM program, 136–138

Skills, for marketing, 25–26, 41, 43, 45

Sligar, Char, on communication, 85

Smith, Heather, on KM assessment, 35t, 37f

Software
  for collaboration, 80–81, 136
  in NASA KM program, 136, 175, 176f

Sowell, Thomas, on species of knowledge, 13

Sponsor, of FAA KM program, 141

Stakeholder community, in aligning KM, 55–56, 65

Standard security work groups, in NASA KM program, 177, 181–182

Status quo, risks of, 57

Stewart, Thomas, on intellectual capital, 16

Storytelling, 195–196

Strategic framework, for measuring KM, 107–109

Strategic needs, for marketing, 33–37, 35t, 37f, 44–45

Strategies
  for aligning KM
    action plan for, 54, 56
    alignment with business strategy, 50–52, 115–117
    based on business model, 48–49, 49f
    current situation analysis and, 53
    development of, 50
  for deploying KM, 78–80

Stress, about future, 4

Subject expertise
  availability of, 38
  mapping of, 57
  marketing to, 24

Supporting role, of KM, 17–18, 125–126

Surveys, of KM outcomes, 100–103, 119–120

Sveiby, Karl-Erik
  on knowledge obtained by doing, 134
  on personnel strategy, 25

SWOT (strengths, weaknesses, opportunities and threats) exercise, 53

T

Tacit knowledge, management of, in Australian Bureau of Statistics, 164–165

Tacit Knowledge Project, for service delivery, 154–155

Target audience, for marketing, 27–28, 39–40, 42, 44

Team Canada mission, to China, 4

Team tables, in Working Without Walls initiative, 169

Team Technology Center, FAA, 138

Technology
  in aligning KM, 49f, 54, 58
  in Australian Bureau of Statistics KM, 158–161
  communication, 192–196
  in introducing KM, 133–134
  in KM usage, 126–128
  in NASA KM program, 184
  support for, in FAA KM program, 142

Telepathy, 196

Templates, for Customer-Facing
    Program, for local
    governments, 153
Terminal Area Operations Aviation
    Committee, of FAA KM,
    140
Testing, in NASA KM program,
    175, 176f
Text messaging, 196
Tool kits
    local intelligence, 150–151
    for policy development, 156–157
    rural intelligence, 155–156
Top-down approach, to deploying
    KM, 73
Touchdown workbenches, in
    Working Without Walls
    initiative, 168–169
Tower Hamlets, London Borough
    of, customer-facing
    program of, 153
Training
    for aligning KM, 54, 65–66
    in Australian Bureau of Statistics,
    161
    for deploying KM, 87, 161
    as metric for KM, 106
    in NASA KM program, 177–179
Transformation Discussion Forum,
    in NASA KM program, 183
Translational processes, unused, 38
Trojan Horse concept, in change,
    17
Trust, for knowledge sharing, 15–16
Turner, Robert, FAA KM
    program, 136, 138

U
United Kingdom
    Knowledge Management
    National Project of, 6–7, 9,
    143–157

Working Without Walls initiative
    of. see Working Without
    Walls
United States Department of the
    Navy, KM metrics of, 96
User accessibility, in NASA KM
    program, 177

V
Value
    of KM, 63, 78
    of sharing knowledge, 85
Value-added activity, KM as,
    40–42
Values, of organization, deploying
    KM and, 76, 83–84
Verification, in NASA KM
    program, 175, 176f
Video nuggets, in NASA KM
    program, 177, 180
Virtual environment, 195
Visible return on investment
    in aligning KM, 54
    in marketing, 24–25
Visual memory prosthetic,
    193
Voice mail, 192

W
Wales, Jimbo, as Nupedia founder,
    194
WebLogs (Blogs), 154–155,
    193–194
WikiLogs (Blikis), 193–194
Wikipedia, 194
Wikis, 193–195
WikiWeblogs (Blikis), 193–194
Wilde, Oscar, on mistakes, 113
Wilkiblogs (Blikis), 193–194
Williams, Robin, 191
Wilson, Woodrow, on change,
    69